Pulcinella

GIORGIO
AGAMBEN

Pulcinella

*or, Entertainment for Kids
in Four Scenes*

TRANSLATED BY
KEVIN ATTELL

LONDON NEW YORK CALCUTTA

Seagull Books, 2018

Originally published as *Pulcinella ovvero Divertimento per li regazzi*

© nottetempo srl, 2015

English translation © Kevin Attell, 2018

Second printing 2020

SERIES EDITOR: Alberto Toscano

ISBN 978 0 8574 2 540 9

British Library Cataloguing-in-Publication Data

A catalogue record for this book is available from the British Library

Typeset and designed by Sunandini Banerjee, Seagull Books

Printed and bound by Hyam Enterprises, Calcutta, India

Contents

Most people think [. . .] that those are philosophers who sit in a chair and converse and prepare their lectures over their books; but the continuous practice of [. . .] philosophy, which is every day alike seen in acts and deeds, they fail to perceive. [. . .] Socrates at any rate was a philosopher, although he did not set out benches or seat himself in an armchair or observe a fixed hour for conversing or promenading with his pupils, but jested with them, when it so happened, and drank with them, served in the army or lounged in the market-place with some of them, and finally was imprisoned and drank the poison. He was the first to show that life at all times and in all parts, in all experiences and activities, universally admits philosophy.

Plutarch,
'Whether an Old Man Should Engage in Public Affairs', pp. 145–7 (1936)

Ubi fracassorium, ibi fuggitorium.

Pulcinella

I

Lying on the grass under the Janiculum Hill, I watch the clouds pass above me. They stand still, change shape, dissolve. This is not how the form of my life has passed. Indeed, early on, I was taken by a desire to search with all my strength whether there were in heaven or on Earth something such that, once I found it, I could eternally enjoy a just and continuous happiness. And I must have remained faithful in some way to this desire if I sometimes seemed to glance at my little patch of sky (as Fabio calls it), even though I certainly had not found it in the places where one usually looks. Indeed, my character was foreign to any kind of ascesis and incapable of denying itself the pleasures and the special joy towards which its tastes inclined, just as an atom in its ceaseless fall cannot escape the clinamen that makes it suddenly swerve. Though I was convinced that it was better to keep the mimes of the comic writers *rather than tragedies under my pillow, the darkness of the times in which I was given to live had constrained me to research that some thought betrayed a rather gloomy soul—which, as my friends know, is clearly untrue. This is why today, having nearly reached my last labour, I would like it not to be toilsome but cheerful and playful, and hope I can show beyond any doubt not only that comedy is more ancient and profound than tragedy—something upon which many already agree—but also that it is closer to philosophy, so close that the two ultimately seem to blur into each other.*

'Plato, it seems, was the first to bring to Athens the mimes of Sophron which had been neglected, and to draw characters in the style of that writer; a copy of the mimes, they say, was actually found under his pillow' (Diogenes 1959: 293[3.1]).

'It is said that as [Plato] lay dying at the age of eighty-one, he had the mimes of Sophron under his pillow' (Valerius 2004: 283[8.7]).

Between the years 1793—when Goya began engraving the *Caprichos*—and 1797—the year of the fall of the Republic of Venice—Giandomenico (or Domenico, as he loved to sign his name) Tiepolo carried out the cycle of frescoes of Pulcinella in the villa at Zianigo, which he had inherited from his father Giambattista and had withdrawn to after abandoning his Venice. When he painted the last two frescoes, *Pulcinella in Love* and *The Departure of*

Pulcinella, he was exactly seventy years old. The room that contained the stories of Pulcinella was not big; it could have been his bedroom, or perhaps a place of meditation. In any case, having reached the last part of his life, he wanted to see only Pulcinella, wanted to speak only to Pulcinella.

PULCINELLA. Che bbuò 'a me? Pecché m'haje chiammato, pecché me scuccie e me custrigne cu' 'na 'nzistaría ca manco 'a tenevano Fiorillo, Baldo e Fracanzano? Vuò ca te cunzolo 'a vicchiaia toja cu' li iucarielle mie? Vuò ca te faccio allicurdà 'o ppassato o te lo vuò scurdare? [What do you want from me? Why did you call me? Why do you bother and cling to me with so much more persistence than Fiorillo, Baldo, or Fracanzano ever did? Do you want me to comfort you in your old age with my *lazzi* (gags, comic routines)? Do you want me to make you remember the past, or forget it?][1]

GIANDOMENICO. Both.

PULCINELLA. Tu vulisse ca pe' 'razia mia 'stu paese—'a vita toja—ca ggià sta teseca teseca, turnasse 'n gagliardía. Nun è chesto ch' bbuò 'a me? [You would like it if thanks to me your city—your life—which is stone dead, came back to life. Isn't that what you want from me?]

---

[1] Pulcinella speaks in Neapolitan. The original edition glosses his dialogue in Italian, which is here translated into English.

GIANDOMENICO. Rather, I need you to detach me from it, to help me serenely let go of it. Not all death is tragic, but every survival is unintentionally comical and this is not the sort of comedy that interests me. And perhaps it is only when something has passed and has seen its time that it becomes truly interesting.

PULCINELLA. 'O ppassato, 'o ppassato. . . . A che te serve 'o ppassato? Je maje l'aggio avuto—chesto vo' dicere 'stu cammesone janco—, pure si ggià tre vvote song' muorto: sparato, 'mpiso e de vecchiummaría. [The past, the past. . . . What use is the past to you? I never had one—that is the meaning of my white smock—even though I've died three times: shot, hanged and dead of old age.]

GIANDOMENICO. What do I want from my past? Memory is the art of not letting the past end and memory is the mother of the Muses. . . . You know, I didn't want life—I wanted more than life. I wanted the indestructible, and that is why I painted. But when life ends, or is about to end, it is as if the indestructible loses its only foothold. Maybe you're right—I want you now. I want that smile of yours that we never see because of your mask. I want to see the indestructible with those eyes of yours which see only gnocchi and maccheroni.

PULCINELLA. Aggio 'ntiso. Tu vuo' l'aternità e ssaje ca je aterno song'. Pe' chesto 'na vota m'haje pittato come a 'nu Giesú Cristo. [I

Giambattista Tiepolo, *Pulcinellas Cooking and Tasting Gnocchi*

understand. You want the eternal and you know that that is what I am. This is why you once depicted me as Christ.]

GIANDOMENICO. Exactly. You are the eternal that does not come before or after time but within it, when everything is or seems to be finished. This is why everything that is within time becomes so light in you, so light.

PULCINELLA. Lieggo comme a 'nu piatto 'e maccarune primma ca tu t' 'o magne. [Light like a plate of maccheroni before it gets eaten.]

'Macarone', 'maccarone', 'maccherone' is attested as early as the seventeenth century in the sense of dimwit, simpleton. According to Albrecht Dieterich, the term derives from Macchus, the character of the simpleton in the Atellan farces. Maccaroni or maccheroni is also the name of Macchus' favourite food, a sort of gnocchi made of flour, cacio and butter, which Teofilo Folengo describes as the foundation of his poetic art: *Ars ista poetica nuncupatur ars macaronica a macaronibus derivata, qui macarones sunt quoddam pulmentum farina, caseo, botiro compaginatum, grossum, rude et rusticanum* [That poetic art is called the macaronic art, derived from macaroni, which are a certain savoury dish bound together with flour, cheese and butter, (a dish) which is thick, course and rustic] (1911: 284). Gulping down the gnocchi, Pulcinella devours his own simpleness.

On 12 May 1797, following the suggestion of Doge Lodovico Manin, the Maggior Consiglio of Venice voted hastily, almost impatiently, for their own dissolution and surrendered the Republic to Bonaparte. In that same year, perhaps in the days immediately following the abdication, Giandomenico decided to dedicate his last labour, the album of drawings titled *Entertainment for Kids*, to the birth, life, adventures and death of Pulcinella. Ippolito Nievo has left us an incomparable description, more worthy of a farce than a tragedy, of that infamous session of the Maggior Consiglio: the Venetian patricians like a 'throng of quivering, shameful, humiliated sheep' who resolve, with just twenty votes to the contrary, to abolish themselves; the Doge, who 'hurried towards his chambers, disposing of his regalia along the way and ordering that his banners be taken down from the walls'; the noblemen who went out into the piazza and 'took care to discard the wigs and robes of the patrician order' so as not to be recognized (Nievo 2014: 435). And the first of the letters of Jacopo Ortis, dated 11 October 1797, by which time Bonaparte was ceding Venice to Austria, shows the grim feelings of those who had had hopes for democracy: 'The sacrifice of our country has been completed: all is lost; and life, if it will be granted us, will serve only to lament our misfortunes, and our disgrace.'

It should come as no surprise that Domenico began the Entertainment *just after the fall of the Republic. The point for him was not, as has been suggested, a flight from reality but the opposite, a closeness to the real and to history that belongs from the beginning to the sphere of the comic. We should never tire of reflecting upon the fact that the comedies of Aristophanes were written at a decisive, indeed catastrophic, moment in the history of Athens. Lysistrata was staged when Athens had just lost, along with its fleet, the flower of its citizenry in Sicily and the enemy, with whom Alcibiades conspired, was just a few miles away. The Acharnians—this comedy that appears so silly—was written when Athens was at war with Sparta, the territory devastated and the peasants amassed in a city where twice the plague raged. Precisely because it carries something metahistorical within it, comedy is intimately involved with history; it bears within itself history's decisive crisis, its judgement.*

Closing himself up at Zianigo in the company of Pulcinella, Giandomenico chooses neither farce nor tragedy. Neither does he choose, as interpreters often claim, disenchantment or disappointment; he chooses, rather, a sober meditation on the end. For in his eyes Pulcinella is certainly—for better or for worse, in disgrace or in glory—that which survives the end of, if not *the* world, at least *a* world—*his* world: the figure that something assumes when it has seen its time. In Christian theology, this figure is recapitulation: 'For the economy of the fullness of time, all things are recapitulated [*anakephalaiōsasthai*] in Christ' (Eph 1:10). It is only through a recapitulation that something—a certain time—can be the 'last', can be said to be completed. Just as it is said that in the moment before death one's entire life flashes—is recapitulated—before one's eyes. Before disappearing, like the ghost of Venice in its liquid sepulchre.

In what way do Venice and the life of Tiepolo recapitulate themselves in the 104 drawings in which the *Entertainment* describes the life of Pulcinella? This is not simply a question of memory. In classical rhetorical treatises, recapitulation is defined as a 'compendious anamnesis of that which has been widely said'. But, on close examination, Giandomenico's Pulcinellan anamnesis resembles more a forgetting that a remembering; it has more to do with laughing and crying than with the archives and registers of consciousness. For him, the fact that in the economy of the end of time all things are recapitulated in Pulcinella implies a new and different experience of history, of life and of time, one that is worth trying to understand.

That philosophy has to do as much with laughter as with tears is attested by an ancient iconographic tradition that represents Democritus laughing and Heraclitus crying. Indeed, laughter and crying are the two ways in which humans experience the limits of language: while in crying the impossibility of saying what one wants to express is painful, in laughter this passes over into joy. Ultimately, however, in the sudden collapse of the facial features and the breakdown of language and voice into gasps and hiccups, laughter and crying seem to blur into each other.

But why does one philosopher laugh while the other cries? The ancient sources suggest that Democritus laughs for the folly of men, who, like aimlessly falling atoms, vainly pursue senseless ends; Heraclitus cries instead for the fleetingness of things that are

Bramante, *Heraclitus and Democritus*

lost in the flux of becoming. In the fresco by Bramante, between the two seated philosophers there hangs a globe. They laugh and cry for what they have seen and grasped of the world. If, however, there is an impossibility of saying at stake in laughter and crying, then this cannot concern what they have understood of the world but the very fact that there is something to understand. That is, it is a matter not of how the world is, but that the world is, the experience not of something that can be said in language but of language itself. That language *is*, that the world *is*—this is not something that one can say; one can only laugh or cry about it (and therefore it is not a question of a mystical experience but of Pulcinella's secret). This is why the two philosophers are shown together: neither laugher nor tears alone, but both at the same time. The viewer should laugh and cry at once.

'He woke up just as dawn was about to break; the roosters were crowing already. He saw that the others had either left or were asleep on their couches and that only Agathon, Aristophanes, and Socrates were still awake, drinking out of a large cup which they were passing around from left to right. [. . .] Socrates was trying to prove to them that authors should be able to write both comedy and tragedy: the skillful tragic dramatist should also be a comic poet' (Plato 1997b: 504–05[223d]).

Spinoza unequivocally stated the motto under which he placed his philosophy: non ridere, non lugere neque detestari, sed intelligere (*'not to laugh at or lament over or despise, but to understand'*) (*2001: 185n24*). *Taking this motto up in one of the aphorisms of* The Gay Science (#333), *Nietzsche seeks to demonstrate that intelligence is nothing other than a certain relation of these impulses—laughter, lament and curse—to one another, similar in some ways to the exhaustion that follows a long melee in a battlefield. Conscious thought, he argues, is nothing other than that part—indeed, perhaps the weakest and least vigorous part—that rises up out of an unfolding process of which we are unaware. It is against this conscious thought, with its seriousness and its 'spirit of gravity', that Nietzsche takes the side of laughter, of the irrational, erratic, careening power that plays with 'everything that was hitherto called holy, good, untouchable, divine' (#382, Nietzsche 2001: 247).*

It is possible, however, that Nietzsche had undertaken this vindication of laughter with too much seriousness, that at a certain point the 'gay science' that he pursued had appeared to him as, in his words, the beginning of a 'great seriousness' wherein 'the real question mark is posed for the first time; that the destiny of the soul changes; the hand of the clock moves forward; the tragedy begins' (#382, Nietzsche 2001: 247.). It is because of this unconquerable remainder of seriousness that in the end Nietzsche, even though he defines himself in Ecce Homo *as a 'buffoon', had to put on the—ultimately stern—mask of Zarathustra and not that of Pulcinella, in which he might have been able to find that happy overcoming of the opposition between laughter and lament that was so close to his heart (1967: 326). And at times it appears to me that if he had chosen Pulcinella instead of Zarathustra, Naples instead of Turin, he just might—in that long winter of 1888–89, when all identity passed away within him—have been able to escape madness. (It has always struck me as a bad omen that in the month of December, just before his collapse, he compared Zarathustra to the Mole Antonelliana.)*

The idea that tragedy and comedy are destined to become one is, in truth, a very ancient one. The term *tragicomoedia* appears in the prologue of Plautus' *Amphitryon*, but the composition of *hilarotragodiai*, 'cheerful tragedies', was already attributed to the Syracusan poet Rhinthon (*c.*300 BC). In both excavated tombs and the paintings of Pompeii, tragic and comic masks appear together. And Plato (who, in the *Republic*, seems to recant his assertion in the *Symposium* and writes that 'Even in the case of two kinds of imitation that are thought to be closely akin, such as tragedy and comedy, the same people aren't able to do both of them well' [1997a: 1032(395a)]) could not have been unaware of the fact that the tragic poets composed those satirical dramas that Demetrius of Phaleron defines as 'playful tragedies' and that they were performed at the end of the tragic trilogy (Demetrius 1902: 149[3.169], modified).

GIANDOMENICO. Does the world make you laugh or cry?

PULCINELLA. Tiene ment' a 'sta mascara; nun vide ca je maje rido e maje chiagno o—pe' meglio parlà—accussí forte astregno

'nzieme 'stí ddoje cose ca cchiú nun se po' dicere: 'È chesta!
. . . 'È chella!' [Take a good look at my mask: don't you see that
I never laugh or cry—or rather, I keep the two so close together
that they can no longer be told apart?]

The question of comedy can be put this way: How can an impossibility of saying produce laughter, be joyful? This is why wordplay and misunderstanding define Pulcinella's relation to language. Pulcinella never understands what is said to him in the sense intended by the speaker:

LUCILLA. You make me so angry!

PULCINELLA. Good! I am hungry too—so let's eat!

And to the priest who asks him to repeat 'Spirit holy and eternal,' he replies: 'Spirit, oil, and tallow.'

In the same way, Totò's rambling speeches are never able to get across what they are meant to communicate. Language does not serve at all to communicate something; it serves, precisely for this reason, only to provoke laughter. Here the 'weakness of language' against which Plato warned in the Seventh Letter has nothing tragic about it; it is openly comical.

To show, within language, an impossibility of communicating and to show that it is funny—this is the essence of comedy.

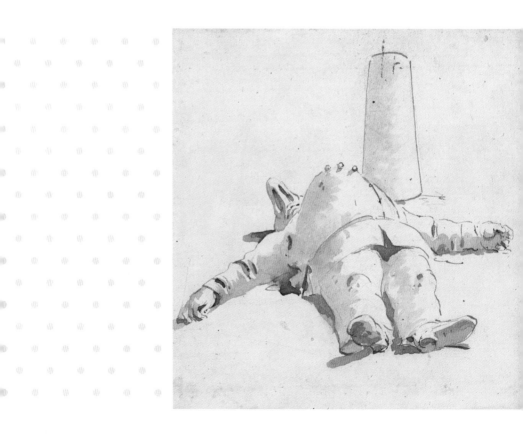

(LEFT) Giambattista Tiepolo, *Drunken Punchinella*

(BELOW) Giambattista Tiepolo, *Two Pulcinellas and the After-Effects of the Gnocchi Feast*

'Tiepolo's Pulcinella', it has been said, was not invented by Giandomenico but by his father. Indeed, in addition to an unspecified number of fragmentary sketches, Giambattista dedicated about twenty-two drawings, two etchings and two oil paintings to Pulcinella. As is the case every time he takes up his father's themes—and he does it often—here, too, it is difficult to imagine two more distant universes.

Giambattista's Pulcinella (except, perhaps, in the two marvellous etchings) is intense, gloomy, essentially 'lumpy' [*gnoccolare*]—a deformed and grotesque body that is constantly cooking, eating, digesting and defecating gnocchi (the festival celebrated in Verona on the last Friday of Carnival is called Gnocchi Friday, which, scholars claim, lies at the origin of Giambattista's drawings). If one thinks of the simultaneously dreamy and triumphant colours of his frescoes and of the haughty, sceptical delicacy of his figures, the black ink (occasionally heightened by a touch of sepia) with which he traces Pulcinella is violent, relentless, almost desperate. Giambattista depicts him at least four times defecting or urinating (in one of the two oil paintings, under a gloomy nocturnal half-light, six Pulcinellas look on as he relieves himself, bluntly turning his gaze towards the viewer). The two drawings that show him digesting with a swollen belly while lying on the ground, once on his back and once face down, have something inhuman and mournful about them. And even when Giambattista paints him in the posture of a river god leaning against a sort of sphinx, the urn that overflows with streams of gnocchi (rather than water) emphasizes the contrast with his ideal mythical model.

There is nothing of this sort in the pages of the *Entertainment*: the life of Pulcinella insistently replays the simple events of a human existence—birth, courtship, marriage, amusements, adventures, work, death. 'Page after page, [Giandomenico] improvises a flowing story, as varied as the hours of life or a chart of the humors: fairytale escapism is interwoven with precise observance of costume; half-obscured "silhouettes," vague shambling figures are pinned on faded backdrops' (Mariuz 1971: 14). Pulcinella's corporeality, which in Giambattista is sordid, becomes tidy and cheerful in Domenico, as if the son had been able to break the spell that had bewitched the hand of the father. This is why, compared to the sharp and sometimes ferocious strokes with which Giambattista styles his Pulcinella, Giandomenico's are 'tremulous, delicate, approximate,' heightened here and there by a touch of white and sepia 'dropped from a dancing hand' (Mariuz 1971: 79). And, in an intentional contrast to his father, Giandomenico establishes a close, undisguised correspondence between Pulcinella's world and the world of myth.

One can see how the father's art and fame might have cast a long shadow on the son. Even in 1972, by which time Giandomenico had been fully rediscovered (thanks in part to the beautiful book by

Adriano Mariuz), and Roberto Longhi, perhaps exaggerating, had declared in his *Viatico* that he was a 'more sincere artist than his father', a monograph on Giambattista could be generically titled *Drawings by Tiepolo*, evidently taking for granted that the son did not exist.

In Giambattista's *Capricci*—for example, in the *Discovery of Pulcinella's Grave*—there frequently appears the figure of an old mage or philosopher wrapped up in a long-sleeved cloak. Similar figures— which scholars sometimes inaccurately describe as 'Orientals'— already appear in Giandomenico's early work in the stations of the *Via crucis* in San Polo. As we know from the testimony of a letter by Pietro Visconti, these 'foreign figures, dressed like Spaniards, Slavs, and other caricatures', disturbed contemporaries because of their incongruence, since 'in that time one wouldn't find those sorts of people, but he put them in because they better suited his character' (Mariuz 1996: 20).

In the *Entertainment*, these figures are precisely reprised by an old man in a turban and large striped cloak who often appears in the foreground and in a solemn pose—as in *Pulcinellas Beside a Villa Wall*, in which this sole human among five Pulcinellas seems to watch, crossly and with his thumbs shoved in his belt, a sleeping Pulcinella. This gesture of holding his thumbs in his belt is exactly what gives us a clue to the character's possible origin, for this is

Giambattista Tiepolo, *Seated Pulcinella Leaning against a Bust*

Giambattista Tiepolo, *Pulcinellas Beside a Villa Wall*

Giambattista Tiepolo, *The Discovery of the Tomb of Pulcinella*

unequivocally the same gesture found in another famous turbanned figure, one who was just as enigmatic for his contemporaries as he has been for posterity: the man standing at the centre of the painting by Giorgione, which in as early as 1525 Marcantonio Michiel called 'Three Philosophers in a Landscape' (1800: 64). The stern, unhurried, attentive watcher of Pulcinella is therefore a 'philosopher'. He can also be seen, this time with his back turned, in *The Prison Visit* and, beside another philosopher, in *The Cattle Sale*. And he is unmistakably there standing beside a crying girl contemplating first the shooting and then the hanging of Pulcinella (just as in the early *Via crucis* he silently watched the ordeal of Christ). Sometimes when he is not present, as in *Pulcinellas at Supper in the Kitchen*, his striped cloak can be seen tossed on the floor in the foreground. It is as if the philosopher's place were always next to Pulcinella, the mute witness to his life.

Today I went back to Ca' Rezzonico for a third look at Gian-domenico's frescoes in the nearly empty halls on the second floor, where they ended up following a remarkable series of removals and purchases. There is no doubt that these frescoes constitute a unified cycle, even if it might not have been conceived as such from the beginning (the first mono-chromes date back to 1759). The surprising correspondence, which I had not noticed before, between the two figures who twirl on their hands in the Pulcinella Room (1797) and the two satyrs who perform the same cartwheel in the Bacchanale with Satyrs and Satyresses *(1771) could,*

Giandomenico Tiepolo, *Bacchanale with Satyrs and Satyresses*

in this sense, be a reference and citation that establishes a connection that had not been thought of at first. The same can be said of the Swing of Pulcinella on the ceiling of the room (1793) and the Swing of the Satyr (1771). The resemblance is obviously not by chance: whether a priori or a posteriori, Giandomenico wanted to give his frescoes a unified meaning.

Contrary to what has been claimed, this is not a 'journey from wildness to civilization' nor 'from the golden age to the present'. The correspondence and interweaving between the different times, and between these times and the timeless, is more complicated than that and seems to me to imply two distinct levels: one mythic and metahistorical (on the one hand, the two rooms with centaurs and satyrs, the staircase with pagan sacrifices and the statue of Abundance and, on the other, the Pulcinella Room); and one historical: the salon-portego with the old world of a dying Venice, exemplified in the sarcastic Minuet at the Villa and Promenade and, opposite them, the great fresco of the New World (1791). The historical world is set, we might say, between two mythic and timeless universes. The two levels, however, are not distinct in time: they both take place—albeit in different ways—here and now, in the rooms of the villa in Zianigo (or as I saw them, in the museum of Ca' Rezzonico). As the old historical world corresponds, in myth, to the semi-feral (or semi-divine) world of the satyrs and centaurs, so too the new world corresponds, in dreams, to the more- or less-than-human world of Pulcinella.

Giandomenico Tiepolo, *Pulcinella and Acrobats*

Giandomenico Tiepolo, *The Swing of the Satyr*

Giandomenico's intuition deserves to be taken up and developed. In the urgency of the times in which he had been given to live, the old painter established a constellation, in the Benjaminian sense, between the satyrs and the Pulcinellas: they contain a secret index that refers them to each other and makes them inseparable. This means that the frescoes at Zianigo entail something like a very special philosophy of history which not only recapitulates and puts into relation two very distant epochs but also substitutes the human protagonists of historical events with semi-animal (or at least not properly human) beings. The last humans, in their outdated fashions, leave the scene in a ridiculous minuet and make room for new, unforeseeable actors: satyrs and Pulcinellas.

The proximity between Pulcinella and the semi-human beings of classical mythology is confirmed by the drawings in which he is abducted by a centaur. This is a reprisal of the theme of the centaur who abducts a satyress, which Giandomenico had earlier drawn in the monochromes at Zianigo. Just like a satyress, Pulcinella seems to be the centaur's object of desire; and the jealous satyr pursuing the abductor and waving a club corresponds here to the three outraged Pulcinellas who threaten the centaur with clubs and sticks.

Giandomenico Tiepolo, *Pulcinella is Abducted by a Centaur*

In granting so much space to the satyrs in the halls at Zianigo, Giandomenico was following a family tradition. In his father's *Capricci*, the satyrs are depicted in their happy domestic context, together with the satyresses and the little ones. Here, as in the frescoes at Zianigo, and in Venetian painting in general (how can one not think of the delightful baby satyr in the foreground of the *Baccanale* that Titian painted for Alfonso d'Este, or of the satyr who, for some unknown reason, holds a mirror up to the sleeping Venus in one of Giambattista's most sensual paintings), the satyrs are half-human, half-goat creatures with hairy lower legs and hooved feet. In this sense, the Marsyas being hung upside down and pitilessly flayed in one of Titian's last paintings is fully a satyr. In Greek vase painting, however (perhaps the oldest example being the François vase which dates from the sixth century BC), the satyrs are originally long-haired and bearded creatures, with visible erections and unmistakably equine legs and tails. The ancient authors tend to conflate them with sileni: 'They call satyrs of advanced age *silenoi*,' Pausanius writes (1971: 66 [I.23.5]), and this information is confirmed by Servius: 'Before growing old, sileni are satyrs' (6.14). In Euripides' *Cyclops*, Silenus is the father of the satyrs (and as such he is called 'Papposilenus', 'grandfather Silenus'). In any case, satyrs and sileni are musical creatures, who end up taking part in Dionysus' dancing entourage, which is alluded to in Giambattista's etchings by the drum and flute left on the floor.

Giandomenico Tiepolo, *Minuet at the Villa*

Many centuries—indeed, nearly two millennia—earlier, a philosopher had made a satyr (or a Silenus) his pre-eminent character. Everyone remembers the comparison Alcibiades makes between Socrates and a Silenus towards the end of *Symposium*. Alcibiades begins by making sure that no one takes this as a joke: 'I assure you my image is no joke: it aims at the truth. [. . .] Look at him! Isn't he just like a statue of Silenus? You know the kind of statue I mean; you'll find them in any shop in town. It's a Silenus sitting, his flute or his pipes in his hands, and it's hollow. It's split right down the middle, and inside it's full of tiny statues of the gods.' Furthermore, not only is Socrates 'just like the satyr Marsyas,' he is also identical to a Silenus in his 'look' [*eidos*] and 'in every other way' [*talla*] (1997b: 497[215a, 215b], modified). Plato also brings up this resemblance in the *Theaetetus* ('snub-nosed, with eyes that stick out' (1997c: 160[143e]), and it must have been a commonplace, since Xenophon also alludes to it: a character in his *Symposium* says that if he looked like Socrates, he 'should be the ugliest Silenus ever to appear in the satyric dramas' (1923: 575[4.19], modified). This physical resemblance corresponds to an essential identity which renders Socrates absolutely heterogeneous to all men who have ever lived and who will ever live ('search as you might,' explains Alcibiades, 'you'll never find anyone else, alive or dead, who's even remotely like him. The best you can do is not to compare him to anything human, but to liken him, as I do, to Silenus and the satyrs, and the same goes for his ideas and arguments'—Plato 1997b: 503[221d]).

Making Socrates—that is, not a man but a satyr or a Silenus—the protagonist of his dialogues (which, as such, even though they are neither tragedies nor comedies, have something to do with the theatre), Plato seems to imply that the subject of philosophy cannot be a human being, cannot be an 'I' or a character like the other personages of poetic storytelling.

In the *Republic* (394c), Plato distinguishes three types of poetic storytelling (*diegesis*): the simple type, as in the poems of Empedocles and Parmenides; the type based on imitation (tragedy and comedy); and the mixed type (epic). The Socratic dialogues are a fourth type, in which the protagonist is not a human but a satyr.

A poetic form in which satyrs play an essential part is the satyric drama (*saturikon drama*), which, beginning with Aeschylus, was performed at the end of a tragic trilogy. This was a *tragoedia paizousa*, a playful tragedy, in which the chorus was made up not of citizens but satyrs. In the *Poetics*, Aristotle claims that tragedy itself must have derived from the actions of choruses of satyrs (*ek saturikou*). In this sense, satyrs are more ancient than the heroes of tragedy, and in replacing—or pairing—human protagonists with satyrs, satyric drama reconnects itself with the non-human origin of all theatre.

It is Plato himself who suggests that the Platonic dialogue, too, can be likened to satyric drama. At the very end of Alcibiades' speech, Socrates describes his friend and suitor's performance in

Dionysiac Frieze (detail)

praise of him as a 'satyr or Silenus play' (Plato 1997b: 504[222d], modified). In this sense, the long encomium for Socrates that Plato stages in his dialogues is also a drama whose protagonist is a satyr. The author, who had begun by recounting the historical narrative of a real man—and thus was writing a very particular type of tragedy—ends up making Socrates a being who is no longer human, the incomparable actor in a satyric drama.

And if the analogy between satyrs and Pulcinella, which guided the imagination of Giandomenico at Zianigo, is correct, then Pulcinella, too, is a philosophical character whose less-than-human, semi-feral or nearly divine story is narrated in the pages of the *Entertainment*.

Ancient comedy preserved its original nucleus in parabasis. The term—which literally means to walk sideways, to deviate, to transgress—denoted the movement in which, after the action had been halted and the actors had left the scene, the chorus took off their masks and, turning directly towards the audience, became once again what they originally were: komos, *a cheerful, tumultuous, insolent Dionysiac procession. In this sense, the parabasis was not merely an interruption or deviation; it was an interruption in which the origin appeared—or, if you like, an origin showed itself shattering and breaking up (the first part of the parabasis was called* kommation, *which meant 'cut') the usual unfolding of the action.*

Giambattista Tiepolo, *Sleeping Venus and a Satyr* (detail)

Despite the stereotypical pretence of a plot, in the comedy of Pulcinella there is only parabasis. Pulcinella does not act in a play; he has always already interrupted it, has always already left it, by means of a shortcut or a byway. He is pure parabasis: an exit from the scene, from history, from the silly, flimsy story in which one would like to contain him. In the life of humans—and this is his teaching—the only important thing is to find an escape route. Leading where? To the origin. Because the origin lies always in the middle [mezzo]; it exists only as interruption. And the interruption is an escape route.

Ubi fracassorium, ibi fuggitorium—where there is a catastrophe, there is an escape route.

Giandomenico Tiepolo, *Pulcinella is Hatched by a Turkey*

II

As his name itself shows, Pulcinella (from *pullecino*: 'chick') is a gallinaceous being, a type of flightless bird; this is also attested by the squeaky voice—similar to Donald Duck's—used by puppeteers when they make him talk. But the etymology is uncertain, since the diminutive of *pullecino* should be *pulleciniello* rather than *pullcinella*, which seems oddly to suggest a female (or at least uncertain) sex. In any case, it is in homage to this etymological tradition that the first pages of the *Entertainment* have Pulcinella being born from a giant turkey egg in a courtyard where the portrait of an ancestor confirms his gallinaceous genealogy.

In the comedy written in 1632 by his inventor Silvio Fiorillo, Pulcinella's full name is given thus: 'Policinella de Gamaro de Tamaro Coccumato de Napole, born in Ponteselice, son of Marco Sfila and Madame Sbrignapriesto,' and later as 'Coviello Cetrullo Cetrulli'. But the name Pulcinella already appears in documents from the fourteenth and fifteenth centuries.

The status of the name is not the same in tragedy and in comedy. '[I]t is only when their plot [*muthos*] is already made up of probable incidents that [the comic poets] give it a basis of proper names, choosing for the purpose any names that may occur to them, instead of writing . . . about particular persons. In Tragedy, however, they still adhere to the historic names' (Aristotle 1984: 2323[1451b, 15–18]). The tragic name is necessary because it traces the fate and the guilt of an individual and not a character; in comedy, on the other hand, the name comes by chance; it is always, so to speak, a nickname and expresses a character and not a destiny. And the character is always innocent. In Pulcinella's case, he has his proper name as a real personage (Pulcinella), but, as a comic mask, he can receive other names at random.

In the *Poetics*, Aristotle provides a definition of tragedy from which we can deduce, by contrast, the definition of comedy that is missing from the book. 'Tragedy,' Aristotle writes,

> is essentially an imitation not of persons but of actions [*praxeōn*] and ways of life [*bion*]. All human happiness or misery takes the form of action; the end for which we live is a certain kind of activity, not a quality [*poiotēs*]. Character [*ēthos*] gives us qualities, but it is in our actions that we are happy or the reverse. In a play accordingly they do not act in order to imitate the characters [*hopōs ta ēthē mimēsōntai*]; they assume the characters [*ta ēthē sumperilambanousin*]

through the action [*dia tas praxeis*]. So that it is the action in it [*ta pragmata*], i.e. its plot, that is the end and purpose of the tragedy. . . . [A] tragedy is impossible without action, but there might be one without Character' (1984: 2320–1[1450a, 14–20], modified).

To understand the definition of tragedy at issue in this passage, let us imagine for a moment that Sophocles' Antigone acts as she does only because she has a certain character (for example, because she is a troublemaker, a contrarian or any other of the characters listed by Theophrastus): the tragedy would no longer be tragedy and immediately turn into comedy. Indeed, in tragedy actions are what is decisive, not characters; in Aristotle's words, the tragic hero does not act in order to imitate his or her *ēthos* but, on the contrary, character is a secondary result of his or her actions—and for this reason could be missing entirely. This is why—that is, insofar as he or she is defined and bound by his or her actions, which can in no way be cancelled—the tragic hero, albeit neither wicked nor immoral, can fall, by error [*hamartia*], into suffering and woe.

The situation of comic personages is the symmetric opposite of this; since they act in order to imitate their character, the actions they perform are ethically indifferent to them and do not touch them in any way. This is why, in their exemplary form, they turn into *lazzi*, that is, into senseless actions and gestures whose aim is solely to interrupt the action and free the character from ever being held responsible. And for this reason Aristotle can write that the ridiculous, of which comedy is an imitation, is a type of 'errancy [*hamartēma ti*] or deformity not productive of pain [*anōdunon*] or harm to others; the mask, for instance, that excites laughter, is something ugly and distorted without causing pain' (1984: 2319[1449a, 33], modified).

In the collection of 73 stage actions transcribed by Domenico Biancolelli, the greatest Arlecchino of all time, he refers to himself always with the formulas 'I do my *lazzi*,' 'I do some *lazzi*,' 'I make the gesture,' 'I repeat this *lazzo* two or three times.' Each time, the *lazzo* is not part of a story, an action in a *muthos*, but, according to the probable etymology of the word, something that slows down and interrupts the sequence of actions, only then to suddenly speed it up. 'While Ottavio talks to his belle, who wants to dress him up as a girl and has taken her skirt off to give to him, I show up and make the gesture of dropping my pants to relieve myself' (Taviani and Schino 1982: 222).

This does not mean that the comic performer enjoys a freedom that is denied to the tragic: he seems, rather, to act according to a sort of mechanical necessity, as if, like Arlecchino, Roger Rabbit or Harpo Marx, he cannot resist doing his *lazzo*; but this is precisely his innocence, that he is irreparably assigned to a character. Since the tragic hero could have acted differently, the error [*hamartia*] consigns him to a destiny and a guilt; the errancy [*hamartēma*] of the comic instead gives him over only to a character.

That someone or something is irreparably as it is: this is Pulcinella. But then the idea of the irreparable, which has been and is so important to me, is in itself comic.

Pulcinella is not a noun; he is an adverb: he is not a *what* but a *how*.

He is neither a character nor an identifiable type: similar to the mask that Pollux calls *panchrestos*, 'good for all uses', he is the underlying collection—hodgepodge, even—of all the features that characterize the personages of comedy.

Tragedy: a destiny that one does not desire but which befalls one because of an error in action, for which one must thus be punished in some way.

Comedy: a character that, like its erring, cannot be set right and does not have the form of an action, but of a *lazzo*.

Character is the comic aspect of fate; fate is the tragic shadow of character. Pulcinella is beyond both fate and character. If character is, as Aristotle says, 'that which reveals the choice of the agents,' Pulcinella has chosen nothing; he is that which has never chosen to do or to be—not even by mistake (1984: 2321[1450b, 8]).

Giandomenico Tiepolo, *The New World*

In the salon at Zianigo, Giandomenico depicted himself alongside his father bemusedly watching the 'new world' prophetically embodied in a technological invention, the cosmorama, which can be counted among the precursors of the cinema. As it should be—since the new does not yet have a face—all the personages—and there are many, of all sexes, ages and social classes—have their backs turned, save the two painters in profile who look on and a baby in the centre (to whom the coming world belongs). The beautiful woman's face—also in profile—that barely pokes out from a white bonnet behind Giandomenico reminds us that always, at all times, there will be a place for feminine charm. On the far opposite side, in exact correspondence to the girl's face and under a white cap that recalls her bonnet, one can make out another face, if in fact it is a face at all: the mask of Pulcinella, which announces the timeless kingdom—or dream—that coincides with the end of the historical kingdom and whose triumph will be celebrated seven years later in the Pulcinella room.

PULCINELLA. Lu munno nuovo è cosa vecchia pe' me, ca l'aggio visto chiú de cientocinquanta vote. [The new world is something old for me, something I've seen a hundred and fifty times.]

What is a mask from the Commedia dell'Arte? Who is Arlecchino? Who is Pantalone? Who are Brighella and the Doctor? Who is Pulcinella?

Pulcinella does not designate a particular artistic personage but rather a *collection of personages*, bound together only by a name, and, up to a certain point, a black half-mask, white smock, and pointed cap. These collections of personages are called, with a rather improper term, *comic types*. But how can we ask and seek to define these collections that are thrown together on the basis of such superficial and external signs? If we try to determine what those personages have in common and proceed by elimination, we run the risk of winding up with nothing in our hands but a name and, perhaps, a costume (Croce 1899: 2).

(Croce's description is inaccurate: in truth the cap is not pointed but cropped. He also seems to accept the image of Callot's Puliciniello in his *Balli di Sfessania* whereas today it is believed that the engraver gave the names randomly.) Only Croce's notorious refusal of any anthropological perspective can explain how name and mask could appear to him as something external and superficial, as if he simply did not know that the 'person', the *rationalis naturae individua substantia*, with which the West has tactlessly branded both the divine and the human, originally just means 'mask' in Latin. Having abdicated all substantial individuality, having remorselessly dropped all personality in order to be wholly and forever only a mask and a name—this really is anything but a superficial undertaking for Pulcinella. Even if he is able do it without exertion and without having to make a decision. He is just as he is, without ever having chosen to be it.

It is already clear to Boethius that the (both theological and anthropological) concept of the 'person' derives from the mask and therefore ultimately comes from the theatrical stage. This brilliant writer, who exerted a decisive influence on Western culture also as a translator, sought a Latin equivalent for the Greek term *hupostasis* which the Greek fathers used to designate the three figures of the single divine substance. Since it seemed to him that the Greek term directly transposed into Latin could be confused with 'substance', he chose to render it as *persona*. '[T]he word person,' he writes in *Against Eutyches and Nestorius,*

> seems to be borrowed from a different source, namely, from the masks which in comedies and tragedies used to signify the different subjects of representation. [. . .] The Greeks, too, call these masks *prosōpa* from the fact that they are placed over the face and conceal the countenance from the spectator. [. . .] But since, as we have said, it was by the masks they put on that actors played the different characters represented in a tragedy or comedy—Hecuba or Medea or Simon or Chremes—so also all other men who could be recognized by their several characteristics were designated by the Latins with the term *persona* and by the Greeks with

prosōpa. But the Greeks far more clearly gave to the individual subsistence of a rational nature the name *hupostasis*, while we through want of appropriate words have kept a borrowed term, calling that *persona* which they call *hupostasis* (1918: 85–7[3.9–23]).

The 'personal' character of the modern subject—at once metaphysical, psychological and political—has its origin, by way of a 'want of appropriate words', in Trinitarian theology; but through this it refers back to a tragic or comic mask. (It is important to note that Boethius, who is dealing with an exquisitely theological question, evokes both tragic personages—Hecuba and Medea—and comic personages—Chremes and Simon.) As a mask, Pulcinella necessarily has to do with a 'personal' problem, and every personal problem is always also a theological one.

Festus says that the ancient actors of the Atellan farces were not obligated, like other actors, to take off their masks on stage at the end of the show (in scena ponere personam) *(1913: 238). This is why they were called 'personati', as if the mask were consubstantial with them.*

The gesture of the modern actor who, like Eduardo De Filippo, takes off his mask or raises it on his forehead after having acted his part is simply impossible for Pulcinella. Pulcinella cannot take off his mask, because there is no face behind it. That is to say, he calls into question the false dialectic between face and mask that has compromised the theatre and, along with it, the ethics of the West. Interrupting this dialectic, Pulcinella liquidates every 'personal' problem, dismisses every theology.

(Although he wore the mask many times, De Filippo belongs to an anti-Pulcinella tradition: that of Eduardo Scarpetta, who had the image of Pulcinella removed from the Teatro San Carlino. When, in his interview with Franco Zeffirelli, Eduardo shows how the immobile black mask can express all passions and all moods, from laughter to tears, from pride to shame, he betrays the essential inexpressiveness of Pulcinella's face, which is so clear in Tiepolo's drawings.)

Eduardo De Filippo during the filming of
Ferdinando I re di Napoli (1959).

A type is a hybrid of uniqueness and generality, an individual trait that becomes the principle of a serial reproduction. As with angels, each of which, according to theology, constitutes a species in itself, so too it is impossible to distinguish in Pulcinella what is unique from what is a repetition. This is why Pulcinella, like Arlecchino, is never alone, is always in a 'mob' [*masnada*]: the *maisnie Hellequin* which is not simply a multitude nor a 'people' [*popolo*] but, rather, a hellish host of demons and ghosts who plunder and destroy everything within reach. Unlike the Arlecchinos, however, the mob of Pulcinellas is peaceful; their favourite occupations are dancing, doing *lazzi* and playing with animals, falling in love, working their trades—in a word, living. A type of people—but an eternal one, without history, like angels or the plebs. And yet, despite the mob, Pulcinella is intimately alone; he watches us unaware of our watching, in 'blinding solitude'. As the gaze of the most regal and ferocious animals is said to be when they encounter a human and seem not to see it.

Not only do uniqueness and generality enter into a threshold of indistinction but also the flesh-and-blood individual and his or her mask. Arlecchino, Pulcinella, Frittellino, Beltrame are not roles played by Domenico Biancolelli, Silvio Fiorillo, Pier Maria Cecchini, Nicolò Barbieri: rather, actor and mask are here called together in a sphere in which real life and theatrical stage fade into each other and lose all identity. Nothing shows this happy contamination between mask and life as well as the way the actors from the

Signatures of actors of the Commedia dell'Arte.

Commedia dell'Arte sign their names: Nicolò Barbieri known as Beltrame, Domenico Biancolelli known as Arlecchino, Pier Maria Cecchini known as Fiorillo—as if the mask were inseparable from their life (it would be impossible, conversely, to imagine contracts signed: Talma known as Oedipus or Eleornora Duse known as Nora).

GIANDOMENICO. If you are not an actor like Fiorillo, nor a mask like Pantalone or Brighella, nor a character like Hamlet, who are you truly?

PULCINELLA. Chi song' je? Songo 'nu penziero! [Who am I? I'm an idea!]

GIANDOMENICO. You mean you don't exist?

PULCINELLA. Te facevo cchiú addutturato de filosofia. Dice Platone ca l'idee asistono, ca esse surtanto overamente asistono. [I thought you were more learned in philosophy. Plato says that ideas exist, that they are in fact the only things that exist.]

GIANDOMENICO. I didn't know you were a philosopher.

PULCINELLA. E je nun sapeva ca tu filosofo nun iri, dopo ca haje tanto strocolato ncopp' a Pulecenella a Ziniago. [And I didn't know that you were not, after all that philosophizing about Pulcinella at Ziniago.]

GIANDOMENICO. You are an idea, but idea of what?

PULCINELLA. Pròpeto chisto è 'o punto: je songo 'na idea senza 'a cosa. [That is the point: I am only an idea, for which there is no thing.]

In Rome, the mask was related to the dead and the theatre: *larva* is both the ghost and the mask of the dead, and this is the name Petronius gives to a silver skeleton 'put together in such a way that the joints and the backbone could be bent in any direction'—a marionette, then, a sort of Pinocchio (2000: 24[34.8]). This leads one to think that the theatre—at least in Rome, but perhaps everywhere—involved a connection to the sphere of the dead, that the stage were a door from which the dead emerged—a *mundus*, as the Romans called the round opening through which the dead, the Manes, passed three times a year to invade the city of the living. The figures who appear on the stage are certainly not alive (indeed, in the case of the tragic heroes they have been dead since time immemorial): only the actors who 'impersonate' them, who put on the mask, are alive.

That Pulcinella has a special connection to the dead is clear from his ghostlike costume: like the *homo sacer*, he belongs to the gods of the underworld, but he belongs to them in such an exaggerated way that he jumps entirely beyond death. This is shown by the fact that it is useless to kill him; if you shoot him or hang him, he always rises again. And just as he is on this side or the far side of death, so too is he in some way on this side or the far side of life, at least in the sense that life cannot be separated from death. In any case, the decisive thing is that a grave figure from the underworld has something essentially to do with laughter.

Flectere si nequeo superos, Acheronta movebo [If Heaven I cannot bend, then Hell I will arouse]: if Acheron is aroused, what comes forth is not the unconscious—it is Pulcinella (Virgil 1999: 1).

Why is it that to make us laugh it is necessary to call forth ghosts and creatures from Hell? How is that a hellish mask can make us laugh? 'This is in no way a phenomenon of decadence, but a regular development: it is for the philosophers to explain it' (Karl Meuli, in Taviani and Schino 1982: 219).

According to folklorists and historians of the theatre, Pulcinella, like Arlecchino and the Zanni, is part of that entourage of underworld figures that accompany the Monarch of the mad, the Biagio or the King of Carnival in the cycle of carnivalesque festivals that, early on in Christian Europe, were substituted for pagan saturnalias whose *insaniae ludibria* [demented mockeries] and *debacchationes obscenas* [obscene ravings] they reproduce. If we laugh and joke during Carnival, it is because laugher, tumult and disorder in some way reproduced the ancient agrarian rites and served to promote the fecundity of the land and the richness of the crops. But what does Pulcinella have to do with this? Obviously he loves to eat and drink,

(ABOVE) Giandomenico Tiepolo, *Pulcinella Before the Magistrates*

(BELOW) Giandomenico Tiepolo, *The Hanging*

but he couldn't care less about agriculture and the harvest. The wild festival usually comes to an end with a formal trial. Carnival is judged and condemned to death as 'insolent, fraudulent, mendacious, voracious, dirty, foolish, shameful, filthy, wicked, mean, lewd, and prodigal' (Toschi 1976: 231). After the sentence, Carnival, personified by a straw puppet or rag doll, is burned, hanged or shot. At times, instead of Carnival being tried and condemned, it is Arlecchino or the 'old Woman.' Or also Pulcinella: 'Carnival is represented,' reads the manuscript of a Calabrian farce, 'in the figure of a short and chubby lout, dressed as a potbellied and humpbacked Pulcinella, with a stringy wig on his head and a bottle and glass in his hands' (Toschi 1976: 217–18).

In the *Entertainment for Kids*, Giandomenico carefully records the arrest, trial, shooting and hanging of Pulcinella. There doesn't appear to be a logical sequence to these events: the drawing in which Pulcinella appears before the judge bears the number 35, but Pulcinella is pardoned and drawings 36 and 37 show him being fêted and carried aloft in triumph by friends and family members. It is not clear, then, why drawing 85 shows him being flogged, which, as with Jesus, happens without a real conviction (in Venice, flogging was reserved for thieves and lazy students), and drawings 97 and 98 show him being shot and hanged. Must we surmise that in the meantime there was a trial that Giandomenico did not want to depict, or that this is a summary execution? In any case, as is clear from the uniforms worn by the firing squad of Pulcinellas and the staff the officer holds in his hand, this is an execution in the name of the law.

Why a trial? Why must the law, in its most extreme and terrible form, intervene in the life of Pulcinella, where it appears as a 'mystery'—the mystery of the trial? Pulcinella, like Pinocchio and Carnival, must undergo a trial, must, like Christ, face a Pilate, who in the tradition of carnivalesque trials is a hulking man 'wearing a topcoat and top hat, with a moustache painted with coal' (Toschi 1976: 235). The essential thing, however, is that there is a judgement, and that this judgement has the form of law. For only after being subjected to the sanctioned forms of law, only after being judged, sentenced and put to death can Pulcinella truly be *as he is.* In the hands of the law, he sheds every substance and every chargeable action: if you believe that I am 'insolent, fraudulent, mendacious, voracious, dirty, foolish, shameful, filthy. . . .' well, then, put on your tragedy, judge me and condemn me for these things that I cannot *be* and whose remains I abandon and hand over to you in the form of *lazzi* and jeers. The *lazzo* is not a chargeable action, it entails no responsibility—it is a pure, irreparable *how*, with neither substance nor moral person. If I am only a character, a signature, a *how*, then I can in no way be defined by or charged with this character: it is what I ceaselessly shed in the hands of the law, without thereby assuming or denying it.

The lazzo makes us laugh because the action of which it consists is cancelled in the very act in which it is achieved. The action that, according to an ancient and venerable tradition, is the place of politics, no longer has a place, has lost its subject and its substance. The comic is not only an impossibility of saying exposed as such in language but also an impossibility of acting exposed in a gesture. But that does not mean Pulcinella is simply impolitical; he announces and requires another politics which no longer has its place in action but shows what a body can do when every action has become impossible. Hence his relevance whenever politics goes through a decisive crisis—for Giandomenico, the end of Venetian independence in 1797; for us, the eclipse of politics and the reign of the worldwide economy. Calling into question the primacy of praxis, Pulcinella recalls that there is still politics beyond or before action.

The anguished political consciousness of his contemporaries Goya and Thomas Rowlandson is often contrasted with Giandomenico's 'sing-song lightness' which takes reality 'with a barely dissimulated touch of heartache' and 'loves the world it depicts and, though it knows its flaws, cannot imagine another one' (Mariuz 1971: 85). But, if it is true that Pulcinella unreservedly and even tenderly adheres to the quotidian, this—if for nothing else but the mask—is raised up to another more inaccessible reality. He is not impolitical—he is, rather, like the man in the chorus of Sophocles' Antigone, 'hyperpolitical stateless' [hupsipolis apolis], stateless because more than political and more than political because 'without a city' (Line 370).

According to Étienne Decroux, the mime is condemned and gagged but his body is free while the actor is condemned and bound to a stake but he is not gagged. Pulcinella is both bound and gagged: he does nothing but say the impossibility of speaking and does nothing but act the impossibility of action. Each time, he bears witness to the fact that one can neither act an action nor speak a word—that *living life* is impossible and that this impossibility is the political task par excellence.

One can act only beyond—or before—action; one can speak only beyond—or before—the word; one can live only beyond—or before—life.

This is why, when facing Pulcinella, the law shows its comic mask; the trial becomes parody, falling always to the side of (*para*) that which it should judge and seize. And the proof is that the rope will not strangle him, the bullets will not wound him, the flames will not burn him. What remains in the hands of the law—and every time slips out of them—is only a man of straw, the rag puppet that was substituted for the true Carnival.

Facilis descensus Averno [easy the way that leads into Avernus], the door is open day and night, *sed revocare gradum . . . hoc opus, hic labor est* [but to recall your steps . . . that is the labour, that is the task] (Virgil 1971: 137[6.126–9]). For Pulcinella this is the easiest thing; he descends and rises, enters and exits from the underworld as he pleases.

It has been suggested that Pulcinella's execution by firing squad inspired Goya's *Third of May 1808,* now in the Prado Museum. At first sight, Goya's oil painting and Giandomenico's ink drawing (probably inspired by an engraving by Callot) would seem to have very little in common, leaving aside the subject and the hardly negligible fact that Tiepolo, just like Goya for Spain, could have been thinking of the executions of the resistors to the French occupation of Venice that began in 1797. Indeed, in the Goya painting, the condemned stand on their feet and gesticulate wildly while Pulcinella, who could be dead or still alive, is tied to a stake, immobile and nearly indifferent. In the background there appears a city which is missing in the Tiepolo drawing. A close examination, however, reveals a significant correspondence: the two bodies of the Pulcinellas stretched on the ground correspond to the three bodies of the patriots who have already been shot in the Goya painting; the gesture of the girl in the foreground covering her eyes with one hand is recalled by that of the horrified witness who covers his eyes with two hands. And a similar violence animates the two riflemen who shoot Pulcinella nearly at point-blank range and the French executioners who are too close to their target. There is, however, a difference: as is clear from the unmistakable hat and mask on top of their regular uniforms, Pulcinella is shot by other Pulcinellas. Beyond the inexorable opposition of their roles, victims and executioners are united in a single, almost ontological solidarity.

Francisco de Goya,
*The Third of May 1808 in
Madrid: The Executions on
Principe Pio Hill*

The genealogy of Pulcinella does not simply go back, as folklorists argue, to the realm of the dead. He is neither dead nor a *larva*, that is, a malign ghost that takes the form of the deceased and infests the world of the living. His relation to death is odder and more complex.

Émile Benveniste and Jean-Pierre Vernant have explicated the nature of what the Greeks called *kolossos*, a puppet made of wood, stone, clay or wax substituted for a missing body in funeral rites and allowing for the re-establishment of the correct relations between the world of the living and that of the dead. That the colossus is not a *larva* or a ghost is proven by that fact that it doesn't look at all like the deceased; it is a vaguely anthropomorphous puppet with joined legs and without, so to speak, a true face, like Pulcinella or Pinocchio. But neither is it a simple substitute for the missing body: indeed, in some cases, one could make a colossus to be substituted for someone still alive. Thus, if the person consecrated to death through the rite of *devotio* had not died in battle as he should have, a 7-foot-high *signum* was buried in his place, and where the image had been buried the Roman magistrate could not walk.

The colossus is, in a certain sense, a fraud: it is a false corpse or a false dead person that is substituted for the real one in order to trick the *larva* and other representatives of the realm of the dead. Pulcinella is a colossus, a non-dead, that stands where a dead person should be, speaks and moves in that person's place and, in this way, mocks and confuses death. He properly belongs to neither the world

 (ABOVE) Giandomenico Tiepolo, *The Firing Squad*

(OVERLEAF) Giandomenico Tiepolo, *Title Page of the Entertainment for Kids*

DIVER

PER LÎ RE

CARTE

of the dead nor that of the living: he is here—irreparably here, in an inaccessible elsewhere. And the wax or straw puppet that is burned or hanged instead of Carnival is in this sense also a colossus—neither a dead person nor a demon. There is a living being where there should be a dead one, and this stubborn, intentional, ironic dwelling in the place of the dead makes us laugh, because it frees us from, lets us cheat, death's double—the *larva* which wanders menacingly in the place of the living. The life of Pulcinella is this life that is for death, not because it is devoted to it but because it comically stands in for it, because it mocks death.

This is why, in the opening of the *Entertainment*, Giandomenico has depicted Pulcinella looking at the sepulchre in which he is buried. He lives next to his own death, stands in the place of his own death, and perhaps the sepulchre that he contemplates is neither empty nor full: Pulcinella is both inside and outside it.

This late drawing parodically recalls the frontispiece of the *Via crucis* from his youth: Pulcinella's tomb, with the inscription *Entertainment for Kids*, occupies the same place as the sepulchre of Christ, which bears the title *Via crucis*. The ladder that in the engraving sticks up from behind the sepulchre is here in the foreground, as if for Pulcinella there had been a crucifixion and deposition as well (the ladder will return many times in the drawings, in particular the first one, where this symbol of the passion, leaning against a wall, is

Giandomenico Tiepolo, *Via Crucis*

DOMENICO TIEPOLO INVENTÒ, PINSE, ED INCISE
Anno MDCCXLIX

Giandomenico Tiepolo, *The Burial of Pulcinella*

present at Pulcinella's birth). Also in the foreground, instead of the cross, shroud, hammer and crown of thorns, lie the emblems of Pulcinella: a plate of gnocchi, a jug of wine and kindling wood. The dog that seems to sniff at Pulcinella recalls his closeness to animal life. More mysterious is the doll that he holds in his right arm, in which it is perhaps possible to recognize the girl with the fan in the *New World*.

In old age, Domenico married a much younger woman. A report of the time, certainly a malicious one, coming from the circle of Canova, describes Domenico as a 'simpleton of the first rank' and then says of the young wife (and of the nephew whom she will marry after Domenico's death) 'this lady has married an old man and to tell the truth she has been sacrificed up to now, for he was surely a good man but full of prejudices, and if he had not had this nephew of his who took care of his affairs this poor thing would have risked suffering the woes of penury.' Perhaps the girl with the fan who so often appears alongside Pulcinella in the drawings of the Entertainment *is precisely 'this lady' (but, if that is true, then Pulcinella is Domenico).*

In a letter of 5 September 1762 to Sophie Vollard, Diderot tells the story of a friend who saw a priest on the streets of Venice who, showing the crucifix to passersby who stopped to watch a Pulcinella show, cried: 'Take no notice of those wretches, gentlemen; the Pulcinella you are flocking to is a feeble fool. Here (the crucifix) is the genuine Pulcinella, the great Pulcinella' (1971: 119, modified).

The Christological references in the *Entertainment* can easily increase: Pulcinella triumphant on a donkey among watching companions certainly recalls the entrance of Jesus at Jerusalem; *The Burial of Pulcinella* (drawing 103) resembles a deposition; and, according to some, even the gnocchi and wine that are always laid out evoke the species of the Eucharistic sacrifice in which the body of Christ is present *vere, realiter et substantialiter*.

The last drawing, with the skeleton of Pulcinella chasing away a group of terrified Pulcinellas, is not, however, a resurrection but a sort of extreme prank. The skeleton seems to want to climb atop a sepulchre that looks rather like a pagan altar (in a previous sketch, the skeleton that tries to climb atop a sarcophagus is that of a monkey).

It is possible here that Giandomenico wanted to mockingly evoke Giambattista's etching *The Discovery of the Tomb of Pulcinella*, in which a semi-nude figure in classical style points to the corpse of Pulcinella with a gesture that recalls that of the shepherds in Poussin's *Et in Arcadia ego*. A sketch by Giambattista, now in the Hermitage—in which four characters (as in the Poussin painting) stoop meditatively above a sarcophagus on which we can perhaps glimpse a number of Pulcinellas carved in relief—seems to confirm the allusion: death is present even in the Arcadia of Pulcinella. The violently burlesque final drawing of the *Entertainment* proves the father's sober wisdom to be wrong: for those who do not know how to die ('je nun saccio murí') but simply die, death is not an object of

Giandomenico Tiepolo, *The Apparition at Pulcinella's Tomb* (detail)

contemplation but of forgetting and fright. Death is always already there in Pulcinella's Arcadia, but as if it weren't.

'Don't be afraid!'

PULCINELLA. Gnornò, je nun tremmo, me spasso a facere 'no minuetto cu' la paura. [No sir, I am not afraid. I enjoy dancing a minuet with fear.]

Giambattista Tiepolo, *Pulcinella Urinating*

III

That Pulcinella has a special life of his own—even, and especially, beyond his appearances on the stage—is precisely what defines the Commedia dell'Arte. We can understand the word 'type', which Croce deems insufficient, only if we remember that the types and masks of the Commedia dell'Arte exist, so to speak, outside the stage or theatre in which they are occasionally evoked. It is as if Pulcinella, Pantalone, Brighella, Rosalinda, and Arlecchino had an existence of their own, from which they can occasionally, perhaps unwillingly, be transported onto the stage, always with the same mask and costume but each time in totally different circumstances and social conditions. Here as a servant and there as a lord, here as a dullard and there very shrewd, even changing sex and number: Pulcinella the bride, the two Pulcinellas—just as, depending on the situation, Pulcinella can be an innkeeper or cook, in love or jealous. . . .

Here, therefore, there is not simply the introduction of stock figures, constantly expressing the same sentiments and always fulfilling the same roles in different plots, as in melodrama; nor is there here the exhibition of definitely limited 'humours' of the Jonsonian sort; rather is there the dramatic presentation of accumulative personalities. [. . .] That they are types in one sense is true, but by their repetition in different circumstances they create the illusion that they are living beings. Had they been merely stock figures, they certainly never would have appealed as they did, nor would they have endured over their stretch of time. [. . .] This discovery of those concerned with the commedia dell'arte was truly a discovery. Although suggestions of its virtue may be found occasionally here and there, the long history of the drama, with the possible exception of early Roman farces, exhibits nothing comparable with it (Nicoll 1963: 22).

Not merely, therefore, types or 'collections of personages,' but creatures that are somehow alive, even if we don't know where and how they pass their life, a life that is unforgettable or always forgotten, stormy or placid, underworldly or heavenly—or perhaps so close that we seem to hear its faint murmur behind a door or in the next room.

This is the only way to explain the curious relationship between the actor and the mask, a relationship which is different from that which usually binds the actor and the personage he or she acts. In a text from the first half of the eighteenth century, *De larvis scenicis et figuris comicis antiquorum romanorum*, the learned Roman Francesco Ficoroni collected the ancient sources on masks. In these sources the actor is often depicted holding his mask, watching and conversing with it. The portraits of the performers of the Commedia dell'Arte, too, show them with the mask in hand, but not looking at it, as if to assert their independence from it and the 'non-coincidence of the two *persons* [. . .], the difference—or tension— between social person and stage figure' (Taviani and Schino 1982: 487). In truth, this is not a question merely of the prestige that the actor, by now fought over by sovereign and lords, was acquiring, but, rather, of the fact that the mask is just as, and even more, alive than he is and that, in taking on its 'person', he, no less than the ancient actors, is traversed by an impersonal and higher life.

In this sense, it is the mask that uses the actor, and not vice versa.

Is not his most proper, most ghostly face in the mask, compared to which the hidden face of the single, private individual X is merely something incidental? The masks serve in order to make the types of the Commedia dell'Arte recognizable, not in the sense of experience and knowledge, but rather insofar as they are members of the archetypal comic condition to which they belong (Kommerell 1952: 171).

Thus, in the portrait of the incomparable Arlecchino Tristano Martinelli (now in the Hermitage), the nobility and seriousness of the face are inseparable from the black mask of Zanni that he displays in his hands. And it is as 'Don Arlequin [. . .] Corrigidor de la bonna langua Francese et Latina, Condutier de Comediens, Connestable de Messieurs les Badaux de Paris, et Capital ennemi de tut les laquais' that he mockingly dedicated to the king of France those *Compositions de Rhétorique*, printed *delà le bout du monde* (this is his true homeland) and consisting only of seventy blank pages and five small engravings. (It has not been noted that the last image perfectly resembles the portrait in the Hermitage, which is proof that this is truly, as we read in a pastel copy attributed to Fragonard, the *portrait de l'auteur et acteur Martinelli*.)

The mask drastically gives the lie to the privilege the moderns give to the face as the pre-eminent place of expression. It is said of Scaramuccia, Molière's teacher, that he once remained on stage for fifteen minutes without talking and that with hand and bodily gestures was able to make the audience laugh. 'You could say that everything in him spoke—his feet, his hands, his head—and that his slightest gesture was created by him deliberately' (Angelo Costantini, in Taviani and Schino 1982: 283). This is the same sense in which David Garrick said of the comic actor's back that it was much more expressive than any serious actor's face.

Tristano Martinelli, illustrations from *Compositions de Rhétorique*

Domenico Fetti, *Portrait of Tristano Martinelli*

The engravings of the *Compositions de Rhétorique* can give us a idea of this 'energetic language' of the body. Even with an immobile body, it presumed—as in Pier Maria Cecchini's comments on Fiorillo, which Croce is unable to understand—'a disciplined clumsiness' and 'an extremely assiduous study in order to go beyond natural boundaries' (Croce 1899: 31). It entailed, that is, taking the most common bodily practices—from one's gait to the way one stands, watches, eats, bends, lies down, sneezes—and 'deforming [them] in an organic way', so that each time, as has been suggested, there is an 'instable equilibrium or *déséquilibre*' among the various part of the body (Taviani and Schino 1982: 486). (Totò displayed a supreme mastery of just such an 'energetic language' in the famous gag of the sneeze in *Totò in Color*.)

'This delightful man has introduced a disciplined clumsiness that, on first sight, chases away melancholy. [. . .] I say "disciplined clumsiness" since he undertakes an extremely assiduous study in order to go beyond natural boundaries, and to show a klutz not far from a madman and a madman who so wants to be near a sage' (Croce 1899: 31).

Above all, contact with Pulcinella entails a transformation of the body. What is at stake, however, is not an Edenic or paradisiacal body that was once lost and is now recovered, but a, so to speak, original that is reached—with discipline, with skill [*arte*]—only later, as a 'clumsiness' or awkwardness. In Pulcinella, the lowliest bodily functions are rendered inoperative and shown as such, and in this way are opened up to a new, possible use that appears as the true and original one. And it is precisely this body skilfully made clumsy that gets a laugh.

Compared to the marionette, which from Kleist to Gordon Craig has provided the model for the actor's body, the body of Pulcinella does not aspire to an Edenic grace to be retrieved beyond consciousness and the Fall, but to a supreme clumsiness like that which Adam and Eve must have displayed when, in a flash of comic genius, they covered their nudity with underwear made of leaves.

Ettore Petrolini: 'The art of the comic is not to imitate, but to deform.' How far can a body be deformed? The double humpback, the belly, the nose. . . . But there is a threshold beyond which the human body truly and irrefutably becomes what it is, what it could never not be: not *my* or *your* body—only *a* body.

Only beginning with the pre-existence of Pulcinella can we understand why the performers in the Commedia dell'Arte lent themselves above all to 'improvised shows'. If we want to understand their art, nothing is more misleading than reading the collections in which they or someone after them transcribed the scenarios for their improvisations. Equally misleading are the general indications that

Giandomenico Tiepolo, *The Triumph of Pulcinella*

Carlo Gozzi used in his wonderful theatrical fables: once writing is involved, even improvisation becomes a 'premeditated show'. At issue is not simply the superiority of the improviser who, 'forgetting something or making an error, is able to recover without letting the audience notice' while the actor, 'who recites like a parrot, is left speechless when he forgets his lines' (Andrea Perrucci, in Taviani and Schino 1982: 255). Rather, the decisive point is that improvisation is possible because the mask of the Commedia dell'Arte already exists and lives before it appears on stage, and the actor does nothing but slip into the life and body—not into a text—of Pulcinella and lets himself be possessed by them. The body of the actor is so 'disciplined' by his becoming Pulcinella that all the rest—above all his speech—cannot be performed in any way but 'on the spot' [all'improvviso].

Nothing expresses the contrast between improviser and actor more clearly than the portraits of the Arlecchino Domenico Biancolelli and of Molière engraved by Nicolas Habert at the end of the seventeenth century: the latter holds a book in his hand whereas the former, with the same gesture, holds his mask. The Commedia dell'Arte can never be a book. This is why the academy of improvisers—called the Eccentrics [Squinternati]—in Palermo had as its insignia a book accompanied by the motto 'Not interned [internati] here,' not imprisoned in a text.

Hence the 'slippages' through which the comic actor can suddenly exit from his part and then immediately re-enter it, as if he
removed his mask and returned for a moment to living his life. It
is, however, difficult to exit from a book; and if you remove its text,
there is nothing left of the character.

Pulcinella not only acts but also lives 'on the spot'. This is why
even though he occasionally practices all the trades (in the *Entertainment*, he takes a turn at being a barber, a woodcutter, a tailor, a
cook, a shepherd, a carpenter . . .), his life is essentially without work
[*inoperosa*]. We could say that the activities he takes up are done seri-
ously and yet in a sort of wager, 'on the spot'. Moreover, no fewer
than 35 drawings show him playing and having fun in all possible
ways (with a shuttlecock, at bowls, with a bird, with dead chickens,
with a giant crab, at the circus, dancing the furlana . . .) with the
same improvised seriousness with which he plies his trades. Two
drawings have him trying his hand as a painter: number 70, in
which he paints an oval portrait of a woman; and another in which
he paints, with a few significant variations, the *Sacrifice of Iphigenia*
that Giambattista had painted at the Villa Valmarana. Father and

(OVERLEAF 1) Giandomenico Tiepolo, *Pulcinella as a Portrait Painter*

(OVERLEAF 2) Giandomenico Tiepolo, *A Dance in the Country*

son—in a certain sense, the whole of Venetian painting—are caught up in becoming Pulcinella.

PULCINELLA. O quanta stelle che stanno 'ncielo! Oh, si me putesse pigliare una de chelle stelle pe' me la 'mpennere a 'stu cappiello! Quanta ponn' essere? Una, ddoje, tre, quatt', cinq', seie, sett', ott', nov' . . . Uh, uh! Quanta, neh! Quanta! Nun 'e pozzo cuntà, se ne porria ènchiere 'nu sacco. [How many stars there are in the sky! O if only I could grab one to put on my cap! How many can there be? One, two, three, four, five, six, seven, eight, nine . . . Ugh! So many! I can't count them. You could fill a sack with them.]

VOLPONE. O what an ignorant fool! Count the stars! Policinella! That's enough! I am going home.

LEIBNIZ. You are right, Pulcinella. No one can see all the stars at once. It is just like when you look at the sea, right here in front of you.

PULCINELLA. 'O mare, 'o mare . . . ma che d'è chistu mare de lo quale tutte quante vanno parlanno? [The sea, the sea . . . what is this sea that everyone talks about?]

LEIBNIZ. Are you joking? In Naples you never saw the sea?

PULCINELLA. Gnornò! A Napule 'o mare nun se vede. [No sir! In Naples you cannot see the sea.]

LEIBNIZ. You are right. In a certain sense, you never see the sea, just as you never see the sky. The perception of the sea, with all its waves and all its reflections, is made up of thousands of miniscule, fleeting, imperceptible sensations. The wave that you see coming is made of movements of the water that are so fine, tenuous and swift that you could never see them. This is why, although the sea is there right before your eyes, it is as if it remained eternally possible—it is the very image of possibility.

PULCINELLA. De gustibus non est sputazzellam, et in secula seculiorum! Comme tu parle a busille! Ma si l'onna te venne 'ncuollo, tu te 'nfracete e si faje 'o summuzzariello, te puo' pure affucà. [De gustibus non est sputazzellam, et in secula seculiorum! How difficult you talk! But if it rushes upon you, the wave will drench you, and if you jump into it you might also drown.]

LEIBNIZ. When you look at the sea, that which is and that which can be, the eternal and the contingent, that which never was and that which is irreparable merge together. This wave that has just now passed and the infinite others that will follow it are irreparably, absolutely what they are, and yet they remain unconcluded, inconclusive, possible. . . . This is the sea: the eternally, irreparably possible—made visible. Do you understand?

PULCINELLA. Ammèn et requie materna! Aggio capito: je song' 'o mare, song' 'o mare! [Amen et requiem aeternam! I understand: I am the sea, I am the sea!]

Giambattista Tiepolo, *Old Pulcinella*

IV

In the story of Er the Pamphylian at the end of the *Republic*, Plato depicts the souls who, arriving from heaven or the underworld 'to a sacred [*daimonion*] spot' before the spindle that sits in Ananke's lap, choose the life into which they will be reincarnated (Plato 2013: 465 [614c]). A herald puts them in a line and, after taking from Ananke's lap a number of lots and models of lives, announces the beginning of another cycle of mortal lives: 'No divine spirit [*daimōn*] will select you by lot, but you will be the one to choose a divine spirit. Let the one who draws the first lot be the first to choose a form of life [*bios*] to which he will adhere of necessity. But virtue has no master [*adespoton*]; by honoring or dishonoring it, each will have a greater or lesser share of it. The responsibility is the chooser's; god is not to be blamed' (475–7[617e], modified). There were all sorts of lives, every possible life, both human and animal: 'There were lives of notable people, some famous for their beauty of appearance and for other strength and prowess; others for their distinguished families and the virtues of their ancestors,' but there were also lives of obscure men and of women of every condition (477 [618b]). And they were all mixed together, full of wealth and poverty, health and sickness, glory or disgrace.

> When he had announced this, [. . .] the first to choose his lot came forward and immediately chose the most absolute tyranny and made his choice through thoughtlessness and greed without considering all its aspects adequately, but what he failed to notice was that in among this it was fated that he would devour his children and commit other evil deeds. But when he thought about it at his leisure, he beat his breast and bewailed his choice and did not keep to what had been said before by the herald. You see, he didn't blame himself for his misfortunes, but chance, the daemons, and everything but himself. [. . .] This spectacle [*thean*] was worth seeing, Er said, how each of the souls chose its form of life: you see, it was pitiful and laughable and astounding [*eleinēn (. . .) kai geloian kai thaumasian*]. For the majority of choices were made through the habit [*sunētheian*] of their previous life. He said he saw the soul of the erstwhile Orpheus choosing the life of a swan out of hatred for the female sex on account of its death at their hands, and so refusing to be conceived and born in a woman. He saw the soul of Thamyras choose the life of a nightingale, and a swan exchange its life for a human one and other musical creatures doing likewise. The twentieth soul chose the life

of a lion. It was that of Telamon's son Ajax avoiding becoming a human being, remembering the judgment of the weapons. After him Agamemnon's soul, also through its enmity with the human race because of what it had suffered, made an exchange for the life of an eagle (481–3[619b–20b], modified).

What does it mean to 'choose a life'? For Plato, the spectacle [*thean*], the 'theatre' of souls who choose models of life is both 'pitiful and laughable' (*geloion*, the term Aristotle uses to define comedy). Choosing a paradigm of a life, each soul in fact chooses its daemon, that is, its character, and the choice of a character cannot but be comic—or better, tragicomic. Life, the destiny that believes it chooses (the choice is actually determined in large part by chance and the habit—*ethos*—of the previous life) is a life that is already packaged (in the first example, the life of that tyrant, in which it is easy to recognize the fate of Tereus or Thyestes, who unwittingly ate their own sons) which the soul can therefore not live but only re-live. To see something like a destiny in the series of events, circumstances and actions that make up a *bios* means not to be able to live it for the first time but only to re-live it. Character is what remains unlived in every life, in the *bios* that the soul has chosen once and for all and is now condemned to re-live according to the decision of Ananke—that is, necessity.

Whoever has a character always has the same experience, because he or she can only re-live and never live. Etymologically, *ēthos* ('character') and *ethos* ('habit', 'way of life') are the same word (the reflexive pronoun *e* plus the suffix *-thos*), and thus both mean 'selfhood'. Selfhood, being-a-self, is expressed in a character or a habit. In each case, an impossibility of living.

What is at play in the relation to character—that is, to the life that has not been lived—is the difference between tragedy and comedy. What is tragic is to exchange the *bios* that has befallen us for a destiny for which we are responsible, thus taking to heart the words of the herald who says that the responsibility lies with the chooser and that god is innocent. This is Aristotle's point when he says that the tragic hero assumes the character 'through the action' [*dia tas praxeis*]: that is, he assumes as a destiny that which he has not lived and cannot live.

The comic character, however, knows that his actions are not important, that they do not touch him in any way, since he performs them only in order to 'imitate the characters' [*hopōs ta ēthē mimēsōntai*]—and this is precisely the point of the *lazzo*: to display the unlived as joking and clowning.

In tragedy, character—the unlived—is transformed into the subject of guilt and destiny; in comedy, character turns into a *lazzo*. The tragic mask expresses the painful assumption of character through

Giandomenico Tiepolo, *Group of Punchinellas with Dancing Dogs,*

actions, the comic its removal through a laughable imitation. The *lazzo* loosens the threads of destiny only to tighten them again in a character. In both cases, however, character—the unlived—remains unsurpassed.

In the story of Er, the only free and truly lived thing is the life that we are able to grasp through virtue—that is, the life that cannot be chosen and drawn by lots, but only loved and desired. Lives are chosen and re-lived; virtue cannot be chosen, only desired. If, in the life that we have chosen to re-live, we are able to reach a point with 'no master'—that is, not chosen but only loved and desired—only then do we truly begin to live, beyond tragedy and comedy, the unlived that is painfully assumed through actions or laughingly imitated in the *lazzo*. This is why the actions and events that constitute *bios* are a matter of indifference up until the moment when we are able to live them 'virtuously', that is, love them and grasp them in a form of life. What is essential is never the life—the series of deeds recorded in a biography—but always and only the form of life, the point at which we are able to live and not re-live character.

To meditate on Pulcinella does not merely mean to ask, like Stendhal, 'What man am I? What is my character?' but also and above all, 'Have I truly lived my life? Or is there still something left in it that I have not been able to live?' This unlived is like a faceless stowaway who accompanies me day after day whom I am never able to catch and speak to.

How much of my life belongs to me, how much to Pulcinella and how much to others? And what does it mean to live with something unlived?

What do we make of that part of our life that remains unlived? A tragedy? A comedy? Or rather, simply, *a* life?

The unlived has two forms: character and phantasm. Character is the guardian of the threshold that ensures that the unlived remains always so, impressing its unmistakable trace on the face (what marks and characterizes our face is not what we have lived but what has remained unlived); phantasm is the attempt to live that which has remained unlived: it always falls short of its goal because the unlived is compulsively evoked precisely and only as something inaccessible. Pulcinella escapes both: character, because he gives up his face for a mask; phantasm, because he entrusts himself only to his childlike forgetfulness.

Pulcinella is the ceremonious farewell of every character; he is able simply to live the unlived without either assuming it as a destiny or comically imitating it. He lives a life beyond any *bios*— precisely the life of Pulcinella that Giandomenico's drawings faithfully present as any and every life [*una vita qualunque*]: he is born, he plays, he falls in love, he gets married, he has a child, he travels, he practices many trades, he gets arrested, he is tried, he is condemned to death, he is shot, he is hanged, he gets sick, he dies, he is buried, and, finally, he contemplates his tomb.

Antonio Maria Zanetti, *A Stout Man Looking at a Puppet Show*

PULCINELLA. E chesta, comme te pare a te, fosse 'a vita mia. M'arrassumiglia, è overo . . . ma forze quaccosa 'nce manca. [And this, you say, is my life? Not that it doesn't resemble me . . . but I feel like something is missing.]

GIANDOMENICO. Take a good look: I think I've put in everything, and even more. All the trades, deeds and misdeeds, dogs, ostriches, centaurs, even the elephant. . . .

PULCINELLA. Nun vulevo dicère chesto, 'nce haje miso pure troppi ccose. 'O fatto è che nun so' securo ch'aggio avuto 'na vita, sinnò je veramente fosse muorto, ma je, ammeno chesto l'haje capito, nunn' jesco a murí, nun 'o saccio fà, je nun saccio murí. 'O fatto è che de quase niente de chello c'haje affiurato je me ne addunaje o, ammeno, nun me l'allicordo. Guarda, pure chill'alifante nun m'allicordo ca l'aggio visto maje e maje song' sagliuto ncopp' 'e rine de 'n'aquila o de 'nu centauro. Strangulaprevete n'aggio magnate tante, ma lignamme, pe' fa' n'asempio, maje n'aggio arrecattato. Ca je, po', song' stato 'nu pittore t' 'o si ammennato 'e fantasia. [That's not what I meant. You've even put in too much. The truth is, I am not sure I have had a life, otherwise I would be truly dead. You have at least understood this—that I can't die, I don't know how, I don't know how to die. The truth is, of all that you have drawn, I feel like I have lived nearly none of it, or at least I don't remember it. Look, even that elephant, I don't remember having seen it, nor did I ever hop on the back of an eagle or a centaur. I've eaten plenty of gnocchi, but I've never, for example, collected firewood. And that I was a painter, well, you've invented that out of whole cloth.]

GIANDOMENICO. You thought that I'd drawn your life, but this isn't a biography. It is—as I've written above—only an entertainment for kids.

PULCINELLA. E pecché a vita mia sarría spassosa? [And why should my life be entertaining?]

GIANDOMENICO. Because I had to draw images, but you lived all that you lived or did not live without ever making an image of it, neither tragic nor comic. This is why you can't remember it.

PULCINELLA. Mò 'nce capimmo. Viva era 'a vita mia quann' nun 'a vivevo. Pe' chesto je nun tengo carattere, nun tengo memoria, Dicímmelo accussí: 'e ccarte meje so' sempe 'n faglia e venco ogne jucata. Sulo 'a mascara mia è 'a faccia overa. [Now we understand each other. I have lived only what I did not live. And this is why I completely lack character. And memory. Let's put it this way: I hold no cards and I win every hand. Under my mask there is no face.]

The question of character finds its most aporetic formulation in the Kantian distinction between the empirical character and the intelligible character. Considered from the point of view of the empirical character, the behaviour of a liar is determined by the

Giandomenico Tiepolo, *The Elephant*

series of circumstances in which he or she is caught up (a bad upbringing, the need to avoid trouble, the desire to please someone . . .) and, as such, he or she is not free. And yet, Kant suggests, if we continue to blame the person who lies, this means that there must be an intelligible character at the base of the empirical one, just as the thing in itself stands at the base of the phenomenon. That is, the choice of the empirical character—or the choice of *bioi* in the myth of Er, which is the same thing—presupposes the choice not of single lies (however grave, however justifiable) but of the intelligible character of the liar.

What is at stake in the Kantian distinction, then, is the attempt to safeguard the freedom of the will at all costs. The intelligible character is nothing but another name for the will. That is to say, the point is to guarantee the responsibility of human actions, to ensure that the subject can answer before the law (both moral and juridical) for that which appears not to be free from the point of view of the empirical character. In the story of Er, in choosing (or believing it is choosing) a life, the soul subjectivizes itself; that is, it subjects itself to a destiny, it constitutes itself as the centre of imputability for its actions (the responsibility is the chooser's). As Schopenhauer will gloss this, pushing the distinction to the extreme: you did not want to tell this or that lie; you wanted to *be* a liar. You are responsible not for what you do but for what you are, even if at the base of this responsibility there is nothing but the pretence that you could have been something other than what you are—that is, ultimately, that you could have chosen another *bios.*

> Freedom belongs not to the empirical but solely to the intelligible character The *operari* of a given human being is determined necessarily from outside by motives, from inside by his character: therefore everything he does happens necessarily. But in his *esse,* that is where freedom resides. He could have *been* another: and in what he *is* resides blame and merit (2009a: 174).

In Schopenhauer's commentary, the aporias that entangle all attempts to ensure the freedom of the will reach their critical mass. The very doctrine that would seek to save responsibility for human actions at all costs in fact ends up identifying freedom with destiny. Through the intelligible character, human beings choose and want what they are, choose not simply single acts but a destiny. This is why Schopenhauer must in the end confess that, for him, too, freedom remains a mystery:

> Thus *freedom* is not removed from my presentation, but merely pushed out, that is out of the realm of individual actions where it is demonstrably not to be encountered, up into a higher region which is yet not so easily accessible for our cognition: i.e. it is transcendental. And this is also the sense in which I would like Malebranche's saying *la liberté est un mystère* to be understood (2009b: 109).

A mystery, certainly—but only if this term is understood in its original meaning of 'theatrical action', *actio,* and therefore 'trial' as well. That responsibility can concern not single actions but one's own being, this is the juridical *monstrum* whose peak is Auschwitz: the Jews—and Gypsies, but ultimately anyone—are responsible not for what they *do* but for what they *are.*

According to this mystery, Pulcinella—every human being—is rightly tried and convicted, because he is responsible for all of his actions—and for the unconsciousness with which he chose them. And not just his soul but also his body, with that absurd double hump and that unbelievable nose, expresses the intelligible character that lies at the base of his being. My body, as Schopenhauer will say, stands to the will in its entirety (that is, to the intelligible character, of which the empirical character is nothing but the manifestation in time) in the same relation as that in which an isolated act of my body (for example, moving an arm) stands to an isolated act of the will; therefore 'individual acts express the same will—that is, the same intelligible character—that the body expresses all at once by its being, only they express it in a succession' (1986: 89). But then even the body is, theoretically, the object of responsibility and of guilt, and ancient physiognomic wisdom, according to which 'as is the will of every living being, so is its body', finds its confirmation and reason for being.

Pulcinella is the critical moment in which the mystery of freedom explodes: the two characters now separate their fates and wander away from each other. Pulcinella's body—his mask—expresses the absolute lack of all will and all character, his being caught at every instant in flagrant, intransigent, blameless abulia. For the 'you must be able to will' that epitomizes the Kantian imperative, he substitutes Karl Valentin's motto: 'I might have been able to want to, but I didn't dare want to.' His gesture is the liberation of the empirical character from any reference to an intelligible character, and of the intelligible character from any function of moral or legal imputation. Between these two unfolds his anonymous, engrossed, carefree life, whose innumerable, unarchivable, unforgettable episodes Giandomenico recounts in the 104 drawings of the *Entertainment*.

The intelligible character, freed of any legal meaning, is an idea: the idea of character. Pulcinella is this idea.

Pulcinella's teaching: I am not to blame for the features of my body, my nose, my belly, my hump. I am innocent of all of it. Ethics begins right after this, but not somewhere else: given this—my?—body, what is ethical is the way in which I live the affection that I receive from being in relation to it, how I renounce or make mine this nose, this belly, this hump. In a word: how I smile at them.

In his final years, Giandomenico seems to have dropped all psychological anguish and all human figures. The marvellous, sparsely scattered birds and hummingbird in flight on the ceiling of the salon of Palazzo Caragiani herald the falconet and parrot of the little room at Zianigo. Birds, dogs, donkeys, deer and fawns, dragonflies, butterflies, centaurs, satyrs and satyresses—and finally Pulcinella. In his white smock, the human tragicomedy is undone and fades away.

Pulcinella's body is no longer, as in Western metaphysics, the animal presupposed to the human. He breaks the false articulation between the simply living being and the human, between the body and logos. The anthropological machine of the West is jammed. This is why his body— at once cheerful and deformed, neither fully human nor truly animal— is so difficult to define. Pulcinella is nothing other than the delight that a body receives from its being in contact with itself and with other bodies—nothing other than a certain use of bodies.

A thin thread connects Giandomenico's *Entertainment* to Giambattista's *Capricci* and Goya's *Caprichos*. And it has indeed been suggested that the *Entertainment* belongs to the genre of the

Giambattista Tiepolo, *A Pulcinella and His Lady*

Photograph of the ceiling of Palazzo Caragiani, Venice.

Giandomenico Tiepolo, Falconet

'caprice'. But does such a genre exit? And in this case can we truly speak of caprices? The term, which indicated the sudden and bold leaping and careening of a goat [*capra*], had earlier been used in poetry and music (Frescobaldi's *First Book of Caprices* from 1624) and then carried over to the visual arts, especially for engravings and drawings. Francesco Alunni's dictionary (mid-sixteenth century) records straightaway its caprine derivation: 'Caprice is the name for a sudden and spontaneous desire, such as that which seems to affect goats, who, when one leaps, all leap.' In this sense, the term could have its iconographic precursor in the bold goat that rises up on its hind legs to nibble at tree leaves in Titian's *Nymph and Shepherd*, whose prehistory André Chastel has traced to ancient sarcophagi and medieval miniatures. The more ancient meaning, documented as early as the thirteenth century in a vernacular translation of Horace, is however 'horror, disgust, dread' [*raccapriccio*] (and only in this sense does Dante know the verbal form '*accapricciare*' [to shudder]: '*e anco il cor me n'accapriccia*' [and my heart still shudders at it] (Dante 2000: 403[22.31]). Horror and goat, *horror* and *hircus* (*horreo* means the hairs standing on end out of fright) are etymologically connected, and this explains the both disturbing and joyful aspect of the 'caprice'. In any case, the simultaneously horrid and bold gesture of the goat provides the model for that of the artist who moves away from the rules of art and reason in order to follow 'the direction of imagination and caprice, in order to entice and please' (Zanetti 1771: 89; the reference is to Giorgione).

Nevertheless, unlike his father and Goya (whose *Caprichos* Domenico bought as soon as they were published in 1799), he prefers to speak of an 'entertainment' [*divertimento*]. Many years earlier, in dedicating a collection of etchings by his father, his brother Lorenzo and himself to Pope Pius VI, he describes the aim of his effort with the term '*trattenimento*' [entertainment]: his intention is to 'serve the pleasure of the numerous amateurs of this not contemptible profession' (see Bostock 2009: 146). These are not, then, 'caprices' but rather—as shown by the care he takes in making the situations more quotidian—simply an 'entertainment for kids'. The pedantry of those who would try to identify these 'kids' among his assistants or actual children of the time is entirely misguided: 'kids' is a generic term for the receivers of the *Entertainment* and entirely in keeping with the subtitle of another book that Giandomenico must have known: Giambattista Basile's *Tale of Tales, or Entertainment for Little Ones* [*Lo cunto de li cunti, overo lo trattenemiento de' peccerille*]. As regards the '*divertimento*', a musical precedent can be found in the sixteen *Divertimenti* that Mozart composed between 1771 and 1779: here, too, we have a series of pieces separated by brief intervals, which have nothing capricious or eccentric about them, so much so that contemporaries saw them as a simple evolution of the 'concerto'.

In 1797, the year Giandomenico began the *Entertainment*, Carlo Gozzi published his *Useless Memoirs*. It has often been suggested that there is a unique proximity between Gozzi's brilliant revival of the Commedia dell'Arte in his theatrical fables and Giandomenico's drawings of Pulcinella. And yet, they are separated by a sort of asymmetric complementarity: in the theatrical fables Pantalone, Brighella, Truffaldino, Tartaglia, and Smeraldina all appear, but never Pulcinella; conversely, Giandomenico knows only one mask. In both cases, presences and absences are certainly not a matter of chance; but why Gozzi had to exclude Pulcinella in particular and why Giandomenico banished all the others is a riddle that is worth reflecting upon if we want to understand the fate of Venice at the end of the eighteenth century.

The coincidence of the dates might suggest another analogy: the *Entertainment*, too, is in some ways a 'useless memoir', that is, an autobiography.

The life of Pulcinella narrated in the 104 drawings—birth, infancy, games, love and marriage, fatherhood, happiness at home, trades, amusements and adventures, voyages, crime and punishment, sickness and death—is also the life of Giandomenico. It is in looking back on his own life that the seventy-year-old painter realizes that he has lived it and that he would like to live it like Pulcinella, without inquiring into its meaning, its outcome or its failure: simply to live it, immediately, immemorially—contemplating it, so to speak, with his eyes closed. And not only to smile, in the

Giambattista Tiepolo, *Dead Pulcinella (Caricature of a Sleeping Man)*

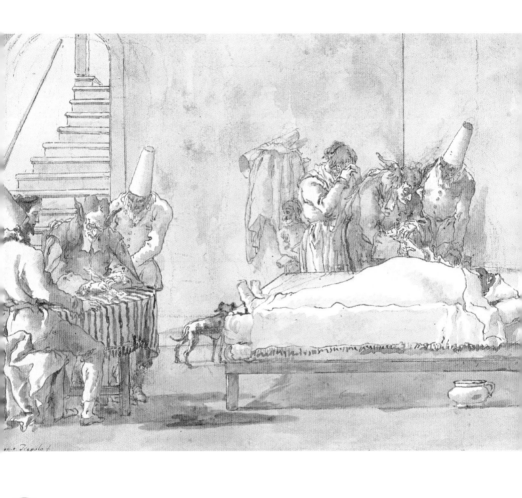

Giandomenico Tiepolo, *The Last Illness of Punchinella*

end, at its absurdity. The secret of Pulcinella is that, in the comedy of life, there is no secret but only, at every moment, a way out.

'I am Pulcinella' is his—and every person's, mine as well—extreme profession of faith. That is: 'I' am not; 'I' cannot live—only Pulcinella can. To live, to make one's life possible, can only mean—for Pulcinella, for everyone—to grasp one's very impossibility of living. Only at that point does life begin. At the point where it becomes true, every autobiography is a biography of Pulcinella. But the biography of Pulcinella is not a biography, it is only an Entertainment for Kids.

Pulcinella—life—is near, very near—and then it goes away, goes away. . . .

It is an—inhabiting—life.

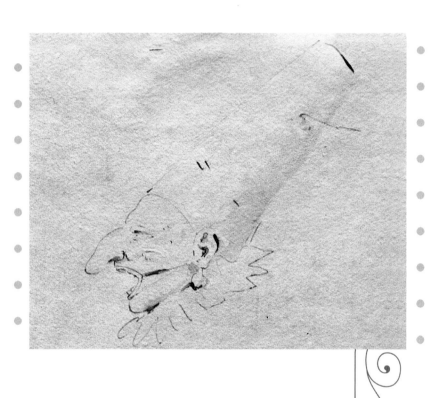

Giambattista Tiepolo, *Head of a Pulcinella*

Postils

At the end of Homo Sacer I, *after evoking a series of brief biographies—
the* Flamen Diale, *the* Homo sacer, *the Führer in the Third Reich, The*
Muselmann *at Auschwitz, the overcomatose person in the hospital
room—in which* zōē *and* bios, *biological body and political body, private
existence and public existence, seem tragically to blur into each other, I
tried to define form-of-life as a* bios *that is only its own* zōē. *But what
can it mean to 'live one's own* zōē'? *What might be a way of life that
has as its object only its own bodily life, which our political tradition has
always already separated out into bare life? What, from this perspective,
is Pulcinella's form-of-life? It is first of all necessary to set aside the* lectio
facilior *that sees him—and every form-of-life—merely as a figure for
natural life, a body that eats, moves, sleeps, feels pleasure and pain, repro-
duces, urinates and defecates. It is a matter, then, of putting in question
and neutralizing the bipolar apparatus of* bios/zōē *itself, in order to
investigate not so much the articulation that keeps them together as the
division that has separated them. That is to say, it will be necessary to
ask in what way and according to what strategies the* bios/zōē *split could
have been produced, and in what way and according to what strategies*

Giandomenico Tiepolo, *Pulcinella as a Trapeze Artist*

it could be neutralized. Indeed, form-of-life, properly human life, is that which renders inoperative the specific works and functions of the living thing and causes them to, so to speak, idle, and in this way opens them up to possibility. In Pulcinella, there is no vegetative life separated from form of life, a zōē that can be distinguished and separated from bios. In truth, he is neither one nor the other. He is, rather, the third term that appears in their coincidence—that is, in their falling together—and, like the trapeze artist in drawing 46 or a tightrope walker who walks along a non-existent rope, he moves freely, with his arduous, disciplined, acrobatic clumsiness, in the space that opens between them and beyond them.

2

*

The puppeteer Bruno Leone has often recounted how his teacher Nunzio Zampella initiated him into the art of the guarattella. *'The 'handwork,' he said, 'is quite easy [. . .] what is difficult is the double voice, that is, the alternation between natural voice and artificial voice' (1986: 12). Contrary to what we might expect, the secret of the art does not consist in knowing how to handle and move the Pulcinella but in being able to produce his unmistakable squeaky voice. And in terms that suggest that here—as in every initiation—there is something like a mortal risk involved, the master insists on the point:*

> *I say that the difficult thing is the artificial voice so that the apprentice of this voice remain on guard toward the dangers that lie in wait: whoever wants to learn it must do it with such a will as to overcome his fear. This is the only way to succeed. It is the artificial voice that distinguishes the Neapolitan puppeteer from any other Italian puppeteer (12).*

The voice is artificial in the literal sense, for it is produced not by altering the voice but by using a small brass instrument, the pivetta, *a sort of flattened coil with a thread wound around it and inside a vibrating* tape (which Nunzio calls a 'spicarella'). The puppeteer must put it in his mouth and make it adhere to the palate, using it like a reed which squeaks and trills according to a special articulation of sounds, all of which is difficult to learn.

The pivetta is the 'true secret of the art,' and yet the master is careful not to teach the apprentice to use it right away.

> I asked Nunzio many times to teach me how to use it, but he withheld it jealously. He told me that his father was the same way even with his children; one time he stole the pivetta from his father's vest and tried it out, and this small theft cost him a beating. [. . .] The meaning of this story was clear: if I wanted to learn I had to work hard and not wait for prompting (13–14).

The aspiring puppeteer got down to work, and after a number of attempts succeeded in constructing a pivetta and tried to use it: 'Just being able to keep it in my mouth was an enormous achievement, even if the articulation and quality of the sound were very poor: I was barely able to make syllables' (13–14).

It was only at this point, when the apprentice had shown himself nearly able to do it by himself, that the initiation occured.

> I went to Nunzio [. . .] the pivetta was the wrong size, too narrow and too long, but it was clear that I had set my mind to it and would go forward. Nunzio looked at it, 'You want to knock yourself out with this? Wait here.' He went into the other room,

picked up a pivetta *that he had prepared for me and gave it to me* (13–14).

Only at this point did the real teaching start: 'Learn to say these words: mamma (which you have to say even though the "m" won't come out with the pivetta*), and then: papà, uncle [zio], that [ciò], shoo! [sciò]'* (14). *Just as when babies learn to speak, the first word is 'mamma'—but this is exactly what you can't say with the* pivetta.

The stories puppeteers tell about the importance of the pivetta *are strangely consistent over time. In London in 1861, Henry Mayhew published the third volume of his* London Labour and the London Poor, *dedicated to the 'street folk'. Among these folk are the puppeteers who set up their little stages for the Punch show (Punch being the English Pulcinella, who was imported from Italy in the seventeenth century. 'The great difficulty in performing Punch,' says a puppeteer in Mayhew's text,*

> *'consists in the speaking, which is done by a call, or whistle in the mouth, such as this here.' (He then produced the call from his waistcoat pocket. It was a small flat instrument, made of two curved pieces of metal about the size of a knee-buckle, bound together with black thread. Between these was a plate of some substance (apparently silk), which he said was a secret. The call, he told me, was tuned to a musical instrument, and took a considerable time to learn. [. . .] He said the composition they were made of was also one of the 'secrets of the purfession.' [. . .] 'They ain't whistles, but calls, or unknown tongues, as we sometimes*

names 'em, because with them in the mouth we can pronounce
each word as plain as any parson. We have two or three kinds—
one for out-of-doors, one for in-doors, one for speaking and for
singing and another for selling. [. . .] My master whom I went
out with at first would never teach me, and was werry partickler
in keeping it all secret from me. [. . .] I was six months in per-
fecting myself in the use of it. I kept practising away night and
morning with it, until I got it quite perfect. It was no use trying
at home, 'cause it sounds quite different in the hopen hair.'

[. . .]

The great difficulty in peeforming Punch consists in speaking
with this call in the mouth—cos it's produced from the lungs:
it's all done from there, and is a great strain, and requires suc-
tion—and that's brandy-and-water, or summat to moisten the
whistle with' (1861: 45, 53–4).

It is quite odd that there is no thematic study on Pulcinella's artificial
voice and his 'unknown tongue', and that we must content ourselves with
information found by chance in works like Mayhew's or a few lines in
histories of the popular theatre. And yet it is this voice that distinguishes
Pulcinella from the other puppets and personages in the Commedia
dell'Arte, not only in Italy but also in England (Joseph Addison compared
the 'Squeak' of his voice to that of a castrato, which he had heard [1711:
n.p.]) and in France, where it was forbidden to make the puppet speak
without the sifflet-pratique (as the pivetta is still called in France).

It is this voice that gives the fundamental characteristic to the show: first because it characterizes Pulcinella, [. . .] gives a power and musicality to his voice and then allows a very strong staccato in the alternation among the voices, giving a particular rhythm to the whole show. At the same time it increases the magical effect of the puppet, which beyond seeming to have a life of its own because of its movements acquires its own voice as well, one that is different from the puppeteer's (Leone 1986: 13).

Pulcinella is not defined, as other puppets are, solely by his character, clothes and cap: he is above all a certain, unique, unmistakable voice. But this voice is not a human voice: it is an artificial being, an 'unknown tongue' produced by the pivetta.

It seems obvious that there is an immediate relation between human language and the voice, even if it is by no means easy to say precisely what the nature of it is. The conventional position here is that the voice of the speaker gives the word a place and a material which allows it to exist and be communicated. Babies learn to speak by inscribing the sounds— the phonemes—of the language that is taught to them into the voice and the memory. Pulcinella calls into question precisely this conventional wisdom. He speaks, even if in a gallinaceous and not always intelligible way, but the language he speaks does not have its place in the voice of the puppeteer. On the contrary, in order for Pulcinella to speak, the puppeteer must lose his voice and diligently learn the 'unknown tongue' of the pivetta. *And he does not loan, as he does for other puppets, his voice, but only his breath and breathing: Pulcinella is 'animated' by the puppeteer in the literal sense of the term—and yet his voice is and remains an artifice, a non-voice. If this artificial voice is the secret of the art, what then is handed down by the puppeteers? Certainly not merely the instrument called the* pivetta, *or* swazzle, *or* pratique, *which in any case is no longer a secret at this point; rather, as the English puppeteer said, it is an 'unknown tongue'. But isn't all poetry—all art—precisely the handing down of a voice and an unknown language that do not belong to us and that we nevertheless produce with childish little ploys, sticking in our mouths a 'flattened coil wound round with a thread'—perhaps 'old, broken-off bits of thread, knotted and tangled together, of the most varied sorts and colors' as Kafka says of the spool Odradek, whose name, he adds, has no meaning in any known language (1971: 428)?*

Bibliography

ADDISON, Joseph. 1711. *The Spectator* 14 (16 March).

ARISTOTLE. 1984. *Poetics* (I. Bywater trans.) in *The Complete Works of Aristotle*, 2 VOLS (Jonathan Barnes ed.). Princeton: Princeton University Press.

BOETHIUS. 1918. *A Treatise against Eutyches and Nestorius* (H. F. Stewart and E. K. Rand trans) in *The Theological Tractates and The Consolation of Philosophy*. London: Heinemann.

BOSTOCK, Sophie. 2009. *The Pictorial Wit of Domenico Tiepolo.* dissertation, University of Warwick.

CROCE, Benedetto. 1899. *Pulcinella o il personaggio del napoletano in commedia.* Rome: E. Loescher & Co.

DANTE. 2000. *Inferno* (Robert Hollander and Jean Hollander trans). New York: Doubleday.

DIDEROT, Denis. 1971. *Diderot's Letters to Sophie Vollard* (Peter France trans.). London: Oxford University Press.

DIOGENES, Laertius. 1959. *Lives of the Eminent Philosophers* (R. D. Hicks trans.). Cambridge, MA: Harvard University Press.

DEMETRIUS OF PHALERON. 1902. *On Style* (William Rhys Roberts ed. and trans.). Cambridge: Cambridge University Press.

FESTUS, Sextus Pompeius. 1913. *De verborum significatu* (Wallace M. Lindsay ed.). Leipzig: Teubner.

FOLGENO, Teofilo. 1911. *Le maccheronee, Volume 2* (Alessandro Luzio ed.). Bari: G. Laterza.

KAFKA, Franz. 1971. 'The Cares of a Family Man' (Willa and Edwin Muir trans) in *The Complete Stories* (Nahum N. Glatzer ed.). New York: Schocken.

KOMMERELL, Max. 1952. *Dichterische Welterfahrung: Essays* (Hans-Georg Gadamer ed.). Frankfurt am Main: Klostermann.

LEONE, Bruno. 1986. *La guarattella. Burattini e burattinai a Napoli.* Bologna: CLUEB.

MARIUZ, Adriano. 1971. *Giandomenico Tiepolo.* Venice: Alfieri.

——. 1996. 'Giandomenico Tiepolo' in *Giandomenico Tiepolo. Maestria e gioco, disegni dal mondo* (Adelheid M. Gealt and George Knox eds). Milan: Electa.

MAYHEW, Henry. 1861. *London Labor and the London Poor, Volume 3.* London: Griffin, Bohn, and Co.

MICHIEL, Marcantonio. 1800. *Notizie d'opere di disegno . . . scritto da un anonimo* (Jacopo Morelli ed.). Bassano.

NICOLL, Allardyce. 1963. *The World of Harlequin.* Cambridge: Cambridge University Press.

NIETZSCHE, Friedrich. 1967. *On the Genealogy of Morals* and *Ecce Homo* (Walter Kaufmann trans.). New York: Vintage.

——. 2001. *The Gay Science* (Josefine Nauckhoff trans.). Cambridge: Cambridge University Press.

NIEVO, Ippolito. 2014. *Confessions of an Italian* (Frederika Randall trans.). London: Penguin.

PAUSANIUS. 1971. *Guide to Greece, Volume 1* (Peter Levi S. J. trans.). Harmondsworth: Penguin.

PETRONIUS. 2000. *Satyricon* (Sarah Ruden trans.). Indianapolis: Hackett.

PLATO. 1997a. *Republic* (G. M. A. Grube trans., rev. C. D. C. Reeve rev.) in *Complete Works* (John M. Cooper ed.). Indianapolis: Hackett.

——. 1997b. *Symposium* (Alexander Nehamas and Paul Woodruff trans) in *Complete Works* (John M. Cooper ed.). Indianapolis: Hackett.

——. 1997c. *Theaetetus* (M. J. Levett trans., Myles Burnyeat rev.) in *Complete Works* (John M. Cooper ed.). Indianapolis: Hackett, 1997.

———. 2013. *Republic* (Chris Emlyn-Jones and William Preddy trans) in *Republic, Books 6–10*. Cambridge: Harvard University Press.

PLUTARCH. 1936. 'Whether an Old Man Should Engage in Public Affairs' (Harold North Fowler trans.) in *Plutarch's Moralia, Volume 10*. Cambridge, MA: Harvard University Press.

SPINOZA, Benedict de. 2001. *Ethica, Book 3, Praefatio*. Cited in Friedrich Nietzsche, *The Gay Science* (Josefine Nauckhoff trans.). Cambridge: Cambridge University Press.

SCHOPENHAUER, Arthur. 1986. *Metaphysik der Natur. Philosophische Vorleseungen, Volume 2* (Volker Spierling ed.). Munich: Piper.

———. 2009a. 'Prize Essay on the Basis of Morals' in *The Two Fundamental Problems of Ethics* (Christopher Janaway ed. and trans.). Cambridge: Cambridge University Press.

———. 2009b. 'Prize Essay on the Freedom of the Will' in *The Two Fundamental Problems of Ethics* (Christopher Janaway ed. and trans.). Cambridge: Cambridge University Press.

SERVIUS, Maurus Honoratus. *Commentary on the Eclogues of Virgil*.

TAVIANI, Ferdinando and Mirella Schino. 1982. *Il segreto della Commedia dell'Arte: la memoria delle compagnie italiane del XVI, XVII e XVIII secolo*. Florence: La casa Usher.

TOSCHI, Paolo. 1976. *Le origini del teatro italiano*. Turin: Boringhieri.

VALERIUS, Maximus. 2004. *Memorable Deeds and Sayings* (Henry John Walker trans.). Indianapolis: Hackett.

VIRGIL. 1971. *The Aeneid* (Allen Mandelbaum trans.). Berkeley: University of California Press.

———. 1999. *Aeneid VII*, 312. Quoted in Sigmund Freud, *The Interpretation of Dreams* (Joyce Crick trans.). Oxford: Oxford University Press.

XENOPHON. 1923. *Symposium* (O. J. Todd trans.) in *Xenophon in Seven Volumes, Volume 4*. (Cambridge, MA: Harvard University Press.

ZANETTI, Anton Maria. 1771. *Della pittura veneziana e delle opera pubbliche de' veneziani maestri*. Venice.

List of Illustrations

PAGE **56** • Figure **19** • Photograph of Eduardo De Filippo during the filming of *Ferdinando I re di Napoli* (1959). Public domain image, available at Wikimedia Commons.

PAGE **58** • Figure **20** • Signatures of actors of the Commedia dell'Arte.

PAGE **62** • Figure **21** • Giandomenico Tiepolo, *Pulcinella Before the Magistrates*, *c.*1797–1804, pen and brown ink and brush and brown wash, with black chalk;   framing lines in brown ink over graphite. The Cleveland Museum of Art, Cleveland.

PAGE **62** • Figure **22** • Giandomenico Tiepolo, *The Hanging*, *c.*1797–1804, pen and brown ink, brown wash, over black chalk. The Cantor Arts Center, Stanford University Museum of Art, Stanford. Public domain image, also available at Wikimedia Commons.

PAGES **68–9** • Figure **23** • Francisco de Goya, *The Third of May 1808 in Madrid: The Executions on Principe Pio Hill*, 1814, oil on canvas. Museo Nacional del Prado, Madrid. Public domain image, also available at Wikimedia Commons.

PAGE **71** • Figure **24** • Giandomenico Tiepolo, *The Firing Squad*, *c.*1797–1804, pen and brown ink, brown wash, over black chalk. Private collection, London. Image courtesy Nottetempo Editorale.

PAGES **72–3** • Figure **25** • Giandomenico Tiepolo, *Title Page of the Entertainment for Kids*, *c.*1797–1804, pen and golden-brown ink, golden-brown wash, over black chalk. The Nelson Gallery, Atkins Museum of Art, Kansas City, Missouri. Public domain image, also available at Wiki-media Commons.

PAGE **75** • Figure **26** • Giandomenico Tiepolo, *Via Crucis*, 1749, etching. Public domain image, available at Wikimedia Commons.

PAGE **76** • Figure **27** • Giandomenico Tiepolo, *The Burial of Pulcinella*, *c.*1797–1804, pen and brown ink, brown and ochre wash, over black chalk. Robert Lehman Collection, Metropolitan Museum of Art, New York. Available at: www.metmuseum.org/toah/works-of-art/1975.1.473/

PAGE **79** • Figure **28** • Giandomenico Tiepolo, *The Apparition at Pulcinella's Tomb*, *c.*1797–1804, pen and brown ink, brown wash, over black chalk. Private collection, New York. Image courtesy Nottetempo Editorale.